DAYLIGHT AHEAD

DAYLIGHT AHEAD

THE DARREN BEADMAN STORY

Darren Beadman
with
Craig Heilmann

K.E.G. Publishing

K.E.G. Publishing
PO Box 1704
Rozelle, NSW 2039
Australia

First published in Australia in 1998

Copyright © Darren Beadman, 1998

All rights reserved. Without limiting the rights under copyright reserved above, no part of this publication may be reproduced, stored in or introduced into a retrieval system, or transmitted, in any form or by any means (electronic, mechanical, photocopying, recording or otherwise), without the prior written permission of both the copyright owner and the above publisher of this book.

Grateful acknowledgement is given for the excerpt from The Sun Newspaper, 9 July 1981.

Design by OMP Design, Auckland, New Zealand
Typeset by Griffin Press, Adelaide, South Australia
Printed and bound in Australia by Griffin Press, Adelaide, South Australia

National Library of Australia
Cataloguing-in-publication data:

Beadman, Darren.
Daylight Ahead : The Darren Beadman Story.

1. Beadman, Darren. 2. Jockeys - Australia - Biography. I. Title

798.40092

ISBN 0 9585870 0 0

I dedicate this book to my loving and devoted family—my wife Kim, son Mitchell, and daughters Jessica and Rachel.

My whole family—every single member of it in their own way— has been an inspiration and encouragement to me ever since I started out as a young colt. They all mean the world to me, I love them with all my heart and appreciate the way they have always supported the decisions I have made in my life. As you read this book you will see how much love and strength can be generated by a family that endeavours to live for each other. You will also see that a jockey's lifestyle is an abnormal lifestyle—what the family had to endure at certain times makes them even more special.

God bless my family. I adore you all.

This book would not be possible without the saving grace of the Lord Jesus Christ of Nazareth.

CONTENTS

	FOREWORD	3
	INTRODUCTION	7
1	*Darkness*	13
2	*Light*	37
3	*Child*	59
4	*Apprentice*	75
5	*Racing*	95
6	*Faces*	115
7	*Winning*	137
8	*Saintly*	155
9	*Why?*	173
10	*Darren's Day*	193
11	*Tomorrow*	211
	EPILOGUE	231
	CAREER HIGHLIGHTS	237
	CAREER TIMELINE	243

FOREWORD

In 1984 I witnessed a young apprentice jockey ride a copybook race to win Australia's premier two-year-old race, the Group 1 STC Golden Slipper Stakes at Rosehill.

Following that important success I closely watched this clean-cut, well-presented young man go from strength to strength, not only as a fine jockey, but also as a human being.

As time went by, I began to use the professional services of Darren John Beadman, and during our early formative years together we had some successes, the most notable being the 1990 Melbourne Cup, with Darren riding the Hains family American-bred import, Kingston Rule.

In 1995 I approached Darren with an offer for him to become a stable jockey for my Leilani Lodge racing stables. Enjoying victories in both Sydney and Melbourne in many of the most prestigious races on the Australian turf calendar, Darren's astuteness, sense of timing and complete professionalism played an important part in our continued success, which culminated in Saintly's Cox Plate/Melbourne Cup double in 1996.

Biblical history books relate that St Paul was very supportive of the athletes of his day, and of the Olympic Games — the running of a race was often compared with Christian life, where the prize is eternal life. Darren Beadman has decided that the 'incorruptible crown that never fades away' is what he wants.

Of course, preachers have often condemned horseracing and gambling. He seems not to have joined that censorious lot, but appreciates his former colleagues, whose respect for him seems to have been increased rather than diminished by his dramatic exchanging of silks and spurs for the robes of religion.

St John Chrysostom — the golden orator — who was one of the greatest preachers of ancient times, and is the patron saint of preachers, tried to reform the social life of Constantinople, of which city he was the patriarch. He condemned the chariot races and the corruption; in his day, these went hand in hand. For all his troubles, he was exiled, and eventually, in his old age, force-marched a long distance. This brought on his death. His body is preserved to this day in St Peter's Basilica at Rome.

It is to be hoped that better rewards await Darren Beadman!

Jesus Christ never rode a horse and, on his entry into Jerusalem on the first Palm Sunday, chose a donkey as his transport. It was a sign of coming in peace. Of course, Darren, as a leading jockey, also must know what it is like to ride a donkey!

So Darren may have to forego some of the joys of horseriding to proclaim a teaching which seems to have brought him peace — and which, he hopes, will bring peace to others as well.

Nonetheless, I would much have preferred he use his God-given gifts in the saddle for a little while longer. I, too, would then have been at peace with the world!

It gives me the greatest pleasure to introduce you to Darren's autobiography, *Daylight Ahead: The Darren Beadman Story*. He is a man who possesses natural gifts, and not only those that helped him reach the top of his chosen profession; with an integrity beyond reproach,

Darren's excellent upbringing and strong family values have stood him in good stead in public life.

His decision to follow the path he has chosen is one more test of his character — which, I believe, will remain unmoved. I wish him well but, had he taken my advice at the time, I would probably not be writing this Foreword!

The door to Leilani Lodge will always remain open to Darren Beadman.

J. Bart Cummings AM

INTRODUCTION

Don't cross your bridges until you've burned them

Dick Bower

I never dreamed that I would be writing a book six months after my retirement, but I have learned over the last few years never to be surprised by anything—and never to take anything for granted; you never know when reality is going sneak up and bite you.

Having been approached by the publisher, I had a few ('quite natural'—he reassured me) fears. I have not been in school for 17 years—well, not regular school, anyway. But now I find myself in a college, studying for ministry, as well as writing this book. I never expected my story to be anything special or worth reporting, but over the years, as I began to win a few races, I found that the media were constantly hovering around asking questions.

Stories, I guess, are like that. They start with questions, and they look for some answers. This story certainly started with a question. Since I announced my premature retirement from horseracing in 1997, people have been constantly asking me: Why?

I hope my book will provide some answers. First, I

wanted to tell people about the events in my life that led to my decision to leave racing in order to study for the ministry. And telling that story really meant going right back and telling the story of my life.

I started racing at fifteen, and had all sorts of dreams and ambitions and I was prepared to work hard to achieve them. What I could never have predicted were the various twists and turns my career would take; nor could I have foretold that at 32 years of age, I would leave the sport that I loved so much.

All in all, my career went well, but some parts of my personal life were messy, complicated, and definitely not what I would have chosen. And in Hong Kong in 1993, I had a particularly trying setback. At this time in my life, I could see my whole 'golden' career just being flushed away—this was a particularly depressing time since I had invested my whole life up till then in getting to the top.

In Hong Kong, I was effectively accused of cheating and disqualified for nine months for 'holding back' my horse. Nobody holds back a horse except for the wrong reasons; to the whole world I looked like a crook. When you have invested great time, energy, and personal resources on staying squeaky clean in an industry notorious (at least in the eyes of the public and the ever-hungry media) for its murky, shadowy personalities, it genuinely stings. Around that time, I became suicidal.

But... (one of my favourite words!) nothing ever has to remain in darkness; there can be light. Because of 'but' I have a story to tell: and that is the story this book is about. I came out of my personal 'valley of the shadow of death' and my life changed. I suppose some people would say that 'I found religion'; I would prefer to say that God found me and rescued me.

I kept racing for a while; but now everything was different. I actually became a better jockey. Maybe I was calmer. Perhaps I had found a reason for being. I stopped asking 'Why?' And I started asking 'What?' What is the purpose of my life? What do You, Lord, want with me? That encounter was the one that encouraged me to abandon racing: to walk away from it all.

I have found a hope and a future. I am now happily married; I have a beautiful family. In racing, I never really valued those things; I took them for granted. You quickly forget, in the cut and thrust of seeking personal glory, that there are people around you who love you and need you to be there for them. Unfortunately, it is so much easier to follow your own road, and just keep on doing the things that are easier for you to do: winning, losing, seeking, and marking your territory. The harder things—giving others time, love, care, compassion; these are the ones that I neglected.

But... God never forgets us. Sometimes we get lucky and get a wake-up call. I was lucky, I suppose—I heard the call.

But this story is not just about Darren Beadman finding God, or being Australia's number-one jockey for a few years. Nor is it about winning Melbourne Cups. It is a story about life itself: relationships, peace, understanding and the mysteries of redemption. This is simply my story: my quiet quest to find peace; tranquillity where there had been turmoil; courage where there had been fear; solace where there had been sadness and tears; joy where there had been grief. This is about the magic of love, the weaving of life's beautiful tapestry, the spoils, not of war, but of peace.

I have found an oasis for my soul in what I am doing. Not many days prior to my sitting down to write this, I visited Redfern to give out donuts to the kids on 'the block'. Nobody in his right mind goes there these days. But I went. First I had to buy the donuts, so I went as usual to the corner store. The owner had seen me in there many times, and asked, 'Darren, what on earth are you buying all the donuts for?' I suppose he thought even past jockeys should not be eating quite so many.

I explained what I am now doing with my time—visiting the kids on the street to offer a helping hand and a little love. He said, 'Mate, you come back any time and take as many donuts as you like.' It costs little to spread a little love; to share with others in need; to say I care.

The pace of life is against us; sometimes it feels that the whole global economic system is, too. And yet, if we fail to grasp the opportunities that do come our way to make the effort to show our fellow Australians that we love them, what hope is there left?

In life, three magical, beautiful words hover together, intersecting and refracting points of glorious light in every life: failure, redemption, and peace. Somewhere, hidden in these words, is stored the treasures of our very selves and of God's mighty love.

1

DARKNESS

If you have raced with men on foot and they have worn you out, how can you compete with horses?

A QUESTION TO THE PROPHET JEREMIAH
JEREMIAH 12:5 (NEW INTERNATIONAL VERSION)

DARKNESS

The second-best punch I ever threw was the right hook that landed squarely on the jaw of the Asian bloke who stole my prize money from the Japan Cup carnival. Apart from that single blow, struck in anger, my time in Hong Kong was a personal and emotional disaster; it landed more body blows on me than I ever deserved or could possibly have withstood on my own. Hong Kong stretched me to breaking point.

I was desperate to make a go of it. I was invited there by John Moore, a trainer, and many other people in the Hong Kong racing industry were also keen to get me over, so everyone was very positive when I accepted the offer. Having won the Melbourne Cup, and virtually every other major race in Australia, I was determined to make good internationally. Only leading international jockeys crack the Hong Kong races—top riders from South Africa, the USA, Ireland, England, New Zealand, France, and many other countries. Hong Kong promised to be the opportunity I had been looking for.

Kim and I had been married for three years and had three kids when we boarded the plane to Hong Kong in August 1992. We had decided to set out a month before racing season began, to give ourselves time to settle in and get a feel for the place. It didn't take us long to find out how strange and intimidating Hong Kong could be for a young and green Australian couple.

But I wasn't going to look a gift-horse in the mouth. Hong Kong was the opportunity of a lifetime for me, and I was going to make it work. I was probably a bit too keen, but I have always had a passion to be the best—running second guts you more than running last does. Hong Kong was my chance to put some really big runs on the board and get the international acclaim I craved.

As things turned out, I did become famous racing in Hong Kong, but for all the wrong reasons.

The Hong Kong racing season kicked off in September, as usual (the season is nine months—September to June—then the industry takes a three-month break). John Moore provided us with a pleasant townhouse out in the New Territories; it was much less cramped for Kim and the kids than anything we could have had elsewhere. With our accommodation sorted out, I was pretty confident that my family was settled for the season, leaving me free from domestic distractions and able to get on with the serious business of winning races. I believed that we were going to be relatively happy there— I certainly was, because my dream was coming true; I was going to have my shot at racing immortality.

But the same could not be said of our marriage. It was on the rocks, and there was a good reason for this. Me. I was selfish. I was 26, and at a stage of my life when all I could think about was myself, my needs, what I wanted. I was so blindly focused on my riding and my career that my family ran a distant second (not by a short half head, but by so many body lengths it was alarming). Racing was my life. Period.

I had no time for Kim or the kids. My priorities were all jumbled up, and I couldn't see what was staring me in the face. I had missed the big picture—my real responsibilities (and I had plenty of them). And Kim and I had serious matters we needed to talk about. We were still only newlyweds, but with an almost instant family— we had three kids under three. Our son Mitchell was born a year after we married and just a year later our twin daughters arrived. The younger one, Rachel, had major medical problems that needed lots of special care and attention. She was born with a cleft lip and palate, and soon after birth was diagnosed as being clinically deaf. Kim and I started to study sign language, thinking, naturally enough, that signing would be our only means of communicating with Rachel.

Though our doctors in Australia, with all their modern medical wisdom, had diagnosed Rachel as being profoundly deaf, God, very early on, performed a miracle in her life that was as stunning as Jesus turning water into wine: Rachel responded to sound after a prayer session at our local church. This miracle was a turning point for us, because we had to decide right then whether she would sign or speak. We decided that no matter what the difficulties, we wanted her to speak. Just before we moved to Hong Kong, when she was still only 13 months old, we began taking her to the Shepherd Centre near Sydney University for hearing training.

When we arrived in Hong Kong, Kim and I took Rachel every week to the top hospital, where we had hired a specialist to give her private speech tuition. But she was so young that she could hardly respond to what was going on. She played up constantly during these sessions because her concentration span was only about five minutes.

Fortunately, Rachel was also too little to know what was happening to us as a family; too young to know what a testing ground Hong Kong was for her parents. How could she know that? And before she uttered even her first word, Hong Kong brought me crashing down.

* * * * *

I threw that second-best punch, an absolutely unforgettable, magnificent right hook, when I was robbed right after I returned to Hong Kong from Japan (I had been competing in the Japan Cup) in 1992. Kim had the car, to take Rachel to the hospital for her speech tuition, and I was looking after Mitchell and Jessica. Because the kids had colds again, I was going to go to the chemist and buy the medication they needed, then meet up with Kim and Rachel at the hospital. As we had only returned from Japan a day earlier, I had a heap of cash (all my earnings) ready to bank, as well as my passport, work visa and credit cards, all neatly stashed in a leather carry-bag.

Kim dropped us off and I navigated Jessica and Mitchell, tandem pram and all, to the nearest chemist, through the crowded streets and markets. You almost never see prams in Hong Kong, because most people carry their children in their arms or on their backs.

We got to a chemist easily enough, but Jessica and

Mitchell were fighting. It was one of those times when a parent has to simultaneously try to tell the chemist what's wanted and separate squabbling kids. To buy a bit of peace and keep the kids at a safe distance from each other, I sat Mitchell on a stool on my right, next to the counter, and left Jessica in the pram near the make-up counter, which was to my left. I put my leather bag on top of the pram while I organised the kids. Mitchell was squawking and producing about as much noise as his little body could muster as I was trying to explain to the chemist what we needed. So while I waited for our prescription to be made up, I went over to comfort him.

As I stood there fussing, a guy, probably about 170 centimetres tall, came up to the counter to ask the saleswoman about make-up and perfume. I noticed that he was asking some pretty odd questions (we were in a part of Hong Kong where most people speak English). What with listening in to his conversation, taking care of Mitchell and waiting for the chemist, I was pretty distracted. I'm not sure why, but I turned around and noticed an Asian guy walk out past the pram very fast. I have no idea why, but the thought immediately flashed across my mind that he'd swiped my bag from the top of the pram. Normally, I would have just grabbed him, but I hesitated, a bit unsure—I should have looked to see if the bag was still there. Then, convinced that he had stolen it, I turned to pursue him. That's when the guy at the make-up counter stepped in front of me to stop me leaving the shop. I sidestepped him, with a move that Peter Sterling in his heyday would have been proud of, and dashed to the door, reaching it at the same time the thief did.

'Hey, mate, you've got my bag,' I said politely and

tapped him on the shoulder as if I was asking him to mind my place in a queue.

I barely finished my sentence. Hearing me behind him and feeling my tap, he bolted.

I gave chase, leaving Jessica and Mitchell in the shop. As soon as I ran after him, mayhem broke out—Mitchell tried to follow me (and fell off the chair in the attempt) and Jessica started to cry. But I knew nothing of this until later on. Like a scene from a B-grade movie, I followed the thief through the middle of downtown Hong Kong, in and out of teeming, bustling streets. I finally caught up with him and grabbed at his back, but as he turned around, he let his jacket slip off in my fingers—a slick move that only angered me further. I pulled it away and gave him my best right hook. It slammed firmly into his chin. He dropped the money and turned to fight.

We grappled like Graeco-Roman wrestlers, all writhing muscles, grunts and groans. Within moments we were surrounded by onlookers, their delighted oohs and aahs accompanying us like a comic symphony as we punched and grabbed. Apparently, they actually thought we were filming a Bruce Lee film, and had pegged me as the bad guy—the evil Westerner!

So there we were, scuffling in the middle of the street in peak hour traffic. In the spirit of a good fox terrier, I held on to him until he regained his feet and threatened a few kung fu-like moves. The onlookers were hooked. Oohing and ahhhing, they watched me throw a few wild punches, not one of which landed.

Normally, there are cops on every street corner in Hong Kong, but at this moment there were none to be seen. The thief, deciding that discretion was the better part of valour, turned tail and fled.

I retrieved my bag and stared down at my ripped shirt, still surrounded by a wide-eyed audience. It felt good to have won. Really good. I thrived on winning. I picked up my bag and his coat and headed back to the chemist's, to find the kids screaming blue murder.

Mitchell had hit his head on the ground when he fell off the chair, and blood was streaming from the wound. The police arrived with their dogs and I called an ambulance to take Mitchell to hospital for an X-ray. Kim called me on my mobile to find out why I wasn't at the hospital—she was pretty shocked when I relayed the events of the afternoon.

Later, when the kids had calmed down and Mitchell was bandaged up, I went to make a police report on the incident. The police quizzed me about whether the thief was Chinese, Japanese, Malay or some other Asian nationality, but I couldn't help them at all with that! I doubt they ever caught those guys, and we never followed it up. Bigger problems followed for us, one after the other, absorbing all our time and energy.

I was victim to two breath-taking and life-threatening falls towards the end of that 1992 season. In mysterious—and inexplicable—circumstances, two horses dropped dead underneath me during races. It was frightening. Up until then I had been going gangbusters. In fact, 1992 had been a bumper season, even by my exacting standards.

The first horse dropped dead in a 1400-metre race on the dirt track at Happy Valley, where there is a run of around 150 metres to the winning post before you turn a sharp corner for the full circuit. Going around the corner for the first time, only 200 metres after the start, I was positioned well and running a strong second. I let the rider in front cross me. In a split second I lost control of the horse. He faltered underneath me, his action lost and his legs wildly flaying.

I tried everything I knew to hold him together so that the other jockey could cross in front of me. I have never been so terrified in my life. Because of my horse's travelling speed, his weight drew him outwards, and then he simply crashed dead underneath me, throwing me up into the air like a rag doll. I fell spine-jarringly on my head and was knocked out cold. By the time the other horses steamed around for the second time and reached the winning post, I had just come to. I had been out for a couple of minutes. I am still baffled about how I lived through that fall, because I came down on my head at 60 to 70 kilometres per hour.

It turned out that my mount had been bleeding internally. The blood pouring out of its nose was clearly visible after it fell, but I had not seen it while riding. My career as a jockey began in 1981, and in more than 11 successful years on the track, I had never had a horse drop dead on me 200 metres from the start. Most racehorses (80 per cent of them) bleed internally, but they bleed at three distinct levels (first-, second- and third-grade). A grade-three bleed (when they bleed from their nostrils) is the worst, but the percentage of horses that die because of that is tiny. This horse had haemorrhaged unusually and inexplicably. I will never be sure about this incident, but someone once told me that cyanide can kill a horse that way.

I was rushed back to the casualty room for X-rays

and then spent three days in hospital in traction. Even though, medically, I only pinched a nerve in my shoulder, the fall and the horse dying spooked me. I gave racing a rest, and Kim and I took off for a 10-day vacation leaving the kids with their Philippino nanny whom they adored. When we returned, I got right back in the saddle. After all, where else was I happy?

I immediately rode a winner. But on the very next ride after that, the mount again dropped dead 200 metres from the start. This horse, like the first, had absolutely no record of bleeding. John Moore had trained the first horse and David Oughton, another Australian, the second, both horses were favourites for their respective races, and both died in exactly the same way. Doubly suspicious. Was organised crime responsible? I will never know, but the coincidences were certainly mystifying.

I only bruised my foot in the second fall, though it was just about as spectacular as the first. I have seen video footage of the falls and they were both truly awful. I can only conclude that stronger limbs than mine were protecting me.

Fearful of what could be going on, John Moore and some of the owners urged me to go home, as there were only two or three weeks of the season to go.

'No,' I said, 'I'm going to ride this out. Someone could be trying to kill me but I don't care. I'm not going to leave the season early.' My determination and pride kept me going. I wanted to win against the odds, so I hung in there for the remaining meetings. Then we came back to Australia for a much needed break during the off-season and just relaxed in our own home in Kensington, generally taking it easy and seeing family and friends.

That 1992 Hong Kong season had been full of personal troubles and horrible falls, so doubtless the entire Hong Kong racing fraternity would have forgiven me if I had stayed in Australia with my tail between my legs. But I saw myself as an international super-jockey, able to leap dangerous conditions in a single bound. In racing terms my 1992 Hong Kong results were very much on par with my performance in Australia—I had 43 wins that season out of 400 races (in Australia I had been averaging around 80 wins in 700 to 800 races). More importantly, I really wanted to keep my word to Neville Begg, a trainer with a stable full of good horses that were likely to produce wins in major races. I had ridden for Neville before in Australia and really liked him as a person. I wasn't going to let him down. And I was still hungry. So we returned to Hong Kong, against Kim's wishes, for the beginning of the 1993 season.

She vehemently opposed going back, but she knew that I desperately wanted to. Hong Kong for me was the big time. Everyone in the racing world was breaking their neck to get there. The dangers of 1992 had not dampened my enthusiasm and, as it turned out, the 1993 racing season was, financially, relatively good to me. This is because the average race in Hong Kong is worth more money than the average Aussie race, so I earned a lot more from my rides. I also won the odd group race throughout the year. By Hong Kong standards, it was a great year.

At home, though, a strange mist enveloped us. Things were going from bad to worse. In the past, during bad times, we had packed our bags to go our separate ways times beyond counting. As the negativity, the hardships and disappointments continued now, though, Kim changed. This time, she grew as a person. Her character altered before my eyes. Though I should have known why, I didn't. On that special day in 1991 when God healed our daughter, Kim, in faith, had given herself to Jesus Christ; Jesus took the reins of her life. So now everything was different for her. One world had ended, and a new life had begun. But I was still blind and selfish, and I just could not see.

I watched Kim being transformed before my eyes, and my frustration and resentment grew. What right did she have to be someone else? (I had no right to blame her for the state of her life. I was the big problem, not her.) In the old days, when things were deteriorating, she had started to drink heavily to cope with the strain. But now, in Hong Kong, she moved in a different direction. She got off the booze. She started to read her Bible. She would go into her bathroom and pray for two, sometimes three hours. She spent most of her time in the bathroom—just being with God. God's Holy Spirit, the power of God that blows on all humans like a loving wind, was turning her into a different woman.

However, this did not fit into the lifestyle that I wanted: we were like chalk and cheese, oil and water. And I handled the changes in her badly—she was a different woman now, nothing like the woman I married. It bothered me to see that she had changed so much; I felt it was abnormal, that she was somehow losing it. Her religion offended me. The Bible was a sharp thorn in my side—it was driving us apart. The harder Kim tried to share her life and faith with me, to share the things that God was teaching her, the more resistant I became.

And she was lonely. In Hong Kong she only had the

kids and God. Where was I? I was functionally absent, the missing piece of the puzzle.

On 28 November 1993 I left home to go to the races at Sha Tin. Kim and I had had a barney at home, and I walked out nursing a foul attitude. My mood was filthy—absolutely the wrong frame of mind for successful racing. I had also been wasting (shedding weight by starvation and sweating in a sauna, which all jockeys do), and had lost two kilograms in order to ride a horse in one of the big local races. Perhaps I had wasted too much, because I blew it. My day was a wipe out.

Race 9 was the Allan Water Handicap—1800 metres, a class three event. (In the Hong Kong racing world there are six classes which refer to the quality of the horses. Class one is the top level). When Race 9 came around, I was on another planet. I was a zombie, and a zombie never knows what he is doing. I certainly did not ride my normal Darren Beadman race, and the stewards pinpointed me for an inquiry.

I spent the rest of the afternoon with Geoff Lane, the trainer of the horse, and the stewards. Time passed, and it got very late, so I rang Kim and told her what had happened. She asked how it looked, and I said, 'Not too good on camera, but I am innocent of what they are accusing me of.'

The stewards claimed that I had not allowed the horse to run on its merits. In all my rides—indeed, throughout my entire career—I had never been questioned on that sort of thing. I had been questioned on careless riding charges from time to time—that happens in competitive racing—but this charge was completely different: it implied illegality, a lack of integrity, possibly even criminal activity. And these guys were trained lawyers and stewards. I walked out of there that day wondering if I had a future in racing—ever. I was very afraid.

The authorities had adjourned the inquiry. A completely new inquiry would be held on the following Tuesday morning at Happy Valley, the administrative headquarters of Hong Kong racing (because the race in question had been at Sha Tin).

When the new inquiry began, I discovered that all evidence taken in the first one (at the track) would be null and void; they were going to start all over again. The stewards also replaced one member of the panel; C H Wong, who had been the race day chairman on the previous Sunday at Sha Tin, was a part owner of our stable and could have been thought to be biased. Apart from the stewards and myself, the trainer, Geoff Lane, and the two owners of the horse, Patrick Iu Po Shing and Dominic Lai, were present.

The inquiry lasted for about four hours. The grilling I received was exhausting and terrifying, the questions endless. It was worse than I had ever imagined it would be. I had to represent myself, and it was awful to feel them all shooting at me. I could see where they were heading from the word go.

My horse, number 13, Better Choice, which raced from barrier 14, had finished fifth in the race, two lengths behind the winner, who had been ridden by Darren Gauci, another Australian rider. (Later I would find out that a huge offshore bet had been placed on Gauci's ride, and because we were both Australians, there was plenty of innuendo that we had been working together.)

The stewards were convinced that something illegal had occurred; that, for financial gain or some other illegal motive, I had not let the horse run to win. Such an accusation—even a whiff of it—leaves a black mark against you not only as a jockey, but also as a person. Your character is on trial. People would always wonder. And innuendo, rumour and gossip are hallmarks of the racing industry; they find fertile soil in any small network or self-contained profession.

The chief stipendiary steward, Mr Hargreaves, began the questioning by asking about my instructions on the riding of the horse.

'My instructions were to…' I hesitated. 'I drew barrier 14 and I was to jump out, come across from barrier 14, and ride the horse quietly and get him back in on the rail. The trainer told me he is a better inside runner.'

He asked Geoff Lane if this were so. Geoff confirmed the instructions. But then the steward began probing Geoff about whether he had explicitly told me to get the best possible placing. Geoff replied that he had. But I had not heard Geoff say exactly those words; I had heard him say to do my best.

Two issues in particular made the stewards suspicious of the ride. I had waited until the 1400-metre mark of an 1800-metre race to get the horse back inside, when Geoff had clearly instructed me to do so early, and I had not pushed the horse enough in the last few hundred metres. I had slapped the horse once with my whip, and I did urge him on, but the stewards felt that I should have been whipping the horse home.

'I did not hear Geoff Lane say to take the best possible position in the race,' I said.

Hargreaves challenged me. 'But what did you assume he meant by "do your best"? What did you assume?'

I was starting to get shaky; the ride was really a blur. 'Assume by... ?'

'By the fact that he didn't say that. Did you make any assumptions?' He fired the question at me.

'At no stage, in all the time that I have been riding, has any trainer or owner mentioned to me to take the best possible position. The normal saying is "do your best". That is... ' Then I was interrupted.

'Well, that or words to that effect, were they said to you?'

'Pardon?' I could not think clearly.

'Well, what you're saying, Jockey Beadman, is that "take the best possible position" was not said, but words of the same meaning were said. Is that what you are saying?'

'No,' I said, confused. 'They said to do my best.'

And on and on it went. They began to grill me about the last part of the race—from 1400 metres to the line. I told them that my horse was starting to quicken at the 1400-metre mark, so I waited to use the whip and simply urged him on with my hands. They were not satisfied with my explanation, and suggested that I had not tried at all.

I told them, 'I was trying to visualise where I was going to get a run between the field. I tried to position him to give him the best possible run to the line. I was trying to look for gaps.'

But they wouldn't buy it. They said that I lost ground at the 1000-metre mark and that from 1400 to 1600 metres out, when I had a chance to go through a clearing, I refused to take it. In fact, at 200 metres from the line I had checked the horse; I was looking for a gap to run into because the horse was a stayer and could not accelerate quickly.

'Do you normally check to make up your mind before you decide where you are going to go?' asked Mr Chew, another panel member.

'At that… at the 200-metre mark, sir, I didn't check. I stopped riding.'

'All right, eased,' he continued.

'Yes,' I said, 'because I was thinking of something; I was thinking of where I was going to go. I didn't want to run up the heels of another horse.'

'Is that a usual trait of your riding? To ease, to think where you are going to go? You've won a Melbourne Cup, Jockey Beadman.'

'Well,' I continued, 'it's a jockey's thing—you've got to think where you are going to go to try to give your horse the best possible chance.'

'Yes. But do you ease a horse when the horse in front of you is three or four lengths ahead? There was a way through and you refused to take it.'

I was starting to wilt under the barrage. 'Well… '

'It seems strange, doesn't it?'

Then the chairman began to press me about why I slowed. 'I don't know why I did it,' I blurted. 'There was just something in me that made me do it, and then… '

'But you've been riding for 12 years. You're not honestly expecting us to believe that you're taking a hold and steadying backwards when you are three or four lengths off horses at the 200-metre mark on a horse that won't quicken and needs to? You're surely not expecting us to believe that?' He could not accept my version of the race.

DARKNESS

In truth, I had not used the whip on the horse because I was not clear what I was doing, and I had slowed the horse because I heard someone near me shout. I wanted to know what was going on before I pushed a gap that only looked like half an opening. But they bought none of it. They made me watch film of the race, grilled me some more, and then asked Geoff Lane about my performance.

One of the members asked Geoff, 'When the horse returned from the race, did you look at him? Did he look as if he'd been in a race?'

'Yes. He was breathing heavily,' he replied, 'and he was puffed out like most horses are after a race.'

Hargreaves asked, 'Taking everything into account, are you satisfied with the ride?'

'Well, I suppose in hindsight, after viewing the race many times, the boy did the right thing in the early part, in my opinion. I suppose in the last 200 or 100 metres he could have used a little more vigour.'

'No,' grumbled Hargreaves. 'Can I have a simple, straightforward answer? Are you satisfied with the ride in all the circumstances that we've gone through?'

'I suppose, having viewed the video, I can't be one hundred per cent happy.'

'Are you happy?' Hargreaves pressed.

'No. Well, no. Especially not the last hundred metres.'

The stewards decided to charge me under rule 131 (i)—not allowing the horse to ride on its merits.

I was permitted to call my own witnesses, but it did no good. Eventually the stewards recalled me and said, 'Darren Beadman, the race meeting stewards have found you guilty…'

I heard nothing more. I was numb. I wanted to speak, but could find no breath. My lungs felt like two empty sacks.

I had tried to hold my head up high throughout the ordeal and tell them I had not done what they were accusing me of, but at this point I just broke down and cried. They told me to go outside and pull myself together.

When I returned to the inquiry room, they handed me a nine-month disqualification. Somewhere in all the gossip and rumour in Hong Kong racing, the authorities must have heard something that painted a false picture. I was innocent, but I had a nine-month ban anyway. Now I would learn what it felt like to be innocent of any crime and still have to pay the greatest penalty—I had to give up racing, and racing was my life.

I walked out of Happy Valley racetrack a shattered man. There is a press photograph of me stepping out of the inquiry towards Kim; my face looks like a death mask.

I stayed in Hong Kong for two more weeks, to appeal the verdict. I was set to ride on a horse called Winning Partners in the International Bowl—a major, world-class, invitation event—during this period. And Winning Partners was the favourite to win. I told the Race Club that I would not ride in an international race, even though, as my appeal had not been heard yet, I could have. I felt it would be wrong, so I relinquished the ride. A knife sliced through my heart when the horse won. (I rode in that race for the next two years—in 1996 and 1997—after serving out my ban, and won both events on different horses.) Those two weeks were the toughest of my life.

New Zealand QC Gary Alderdice put together my submission. I quickly collected references from Bart

Cummings, Theo Green, Ron Quinton, the Ingham brothers, Lee Freedman, and even John Tapp, to reinforce the credibility of my appeal. Theo Green, who was sick in hospital at the time, wrote telling the Royal Hong Kong Jockey Club that excessive wasting impairs my judgement in a race. Ron Quinton confirmed this: 'Theo Green told me of his concern whenever Darren did any significant and rapid wasting. This concern became more focused over the years, resulting in an incident at Randwick several years ago, when he forced Darren to dismount in the saddling paddock and replaced him with another jockey. From time to time I have also noticed Darren's obvious stress, both in appearance and attitude, when he wastes excessively.'

Lee Freedman's reference summed up how I felt: 'When a person's character is called into question, many people react negatively and believe there must be something in the rumour and innuendo.' But then he added: 'I would say, however, in Darren Beadman's case, that my opinion of him would be as high now as it ever has been in the past.' That meant a lot to me.

But my appeal was rejected, and in the end, the legal fees also crippled me; they ran into hundreds of thousands of Hong Kong dollars in just a few weeks (around $40 thousand Australian dollars).

In the two weeks between the disqualification and the appeal, the Hong Kong Jockey Club summoned me again and insisted that they knew five reasons for me holding my horse back. The stewards were adamant that I was either working with another jockey, or I did it myself, or I was working with a trainer or with punters, or somebody paid me to do it. I denied all those suggestions:

'It is none of the five, so I can't help you.'

'If you're willing to help us, we'll reduce your sentence—we really want to know what's going on here,' they offered.

But I had to keep saying, 'I can't help you.' How could I help them? There was nothing to tell—no secret plot, no villains, no under-the-counter money.

Even after I had returned to Australia, I was asked to go back to Hong Kong several times to give evidence. In February 1994 the head of security at the Hong Kong Jockey club offered me an all-expenses paid trip to tell them everything I knew. 'No one will know you're here,' he promised. 'I am determined to get to the bottom of this.' But I declined and handed the matter over to Gary Alderdice. The authorities had cracked something, and they thought I was part of it, but they were wrong. I did not pull the horse. There was no conspiracy; it was just a lousy ride.

*****

Throughout the Hong Kong ordeal, and even though we had been having desperate family and marriage troubles, Kim came to my aid time and time again, and tried to help me through the pain. I watched her grow and change in ways I could not understand and she pulled me through those nine months as nobody else could have. Nine months—the gestation time for a baby. Nine months—preparing for birth. And so it would be with me. In the end that ban brought about a rebirth.

After Hong Kong, I hit rock bottom during the ban. It is a cliché, but true, to say that I really thought my life was over. Racing was all I knew, and now I was out—I couldn't go near any racetrack in the world nor could I 'consort' with any of my friends, and as I only had friends in racing, I was totally alone. I wasn't even sure there would ever be another open door in racing: it is almost impossible to bounce back from the stigma of the charge for which I received the ban. Who could trust me? Who would want to? Plenty of jockeys had failed to come back from such a ban. What would happen to me?

Hong Kong signified my darkest hour; but I would emerge into the light.

2

LIGHT

...Saul kept up his violent threats of murder against the followers of the Lord. He went to the High Priest and asked for letters of introduction to the synagogues in Damascus, so that if he should find there any followers of the Way of the Lord, he would be able to arrest them, both men and women, and bring them back to Jerusalem.
As Saul was approaching the city of Damascus, suddenly a light from the sky flashed around him. He fell to the ground and heard a voice saying to him, 'Saul, Saul! Why do you persecute me?'
'Who are you, Lord?' he asked.
'I am Jesus, whom you persecute,' the voice said. 'But get up and go into the city, where you will be told what to do.'
...Saul got up from the ground and opened his eyes, but could not see a thing. So they took him by the hand and led him to Damascus. For three days he was not able to see, and during that time he did not eat or drink anything.
'...I have chosen him to serve me, to make my name known to Gentiles and kings and to the people of Israel. And I myself will show him all that he must suffer for my sake.'

THE CONVERSION OF SAUL,
ACTS 9.1–9.15 (GOOD NEWS BIBLE)

LIGHT

Finding True North on the compass of my life began in March 1991, when doctors diagnosed hydrocephalus in our daughter Rachel before she was born. To compound matters, she was born with a cleft lip and palate, and shortly after her birth, our specialist physician, Professor Gibson, diagnosed her as being profoundly deaf. Because of the hydrocephalus, the surgeons inserted two shunts into her brain during her first two months in hospital.

Rachel was born on 5 March into the sterile world of Camperdown Children's Hospital in less than perfect circumstances, and with her future looking grim.

Kim and I were busy raising a feisty 11-month old son, Mitchell, when our little miracles—our twins, Jessica and Rachel—appeared on the scene. Things immediately became extremely difficult for us to cope with. We were relatively young—both only 24 years old—and, because Mitchell's birth had gone well, we had been taking everything for granted. Mitchell was a healthy, happy, bouncing baby boy, so when Kim was pregnant with the girls, there seemed every reason to assume the best. Why would we expect any problems, let alone major ones?

I remember the day we first found out there were complications with the pregnancy. Kim was 34 weeks pregnant, and we knew we were expecting twins. She had her scheduled ultrasound on Monday (4 March), and was then to return to the doctor's office the following day to hear the results. I had been riding track work in the morning and had returned home to sweat in the sauna; the phone was off the hook, which meant Kim couldn't reach me with the news.

It was a beautiful, sunny autumn day I remember. I was just out of the sauna when a neighbour arrived at our house and knocked loudly on the door. 'What's wrong?' I asked, surprised.

'You need to call Kim at your doctor's office and cancel your race rides for the day,' she said. It sounded pretty serious, so I just jumped into the car and rang Kim as I drove to the doctor's rooms to see what the matter was. Kim sounded as though she was in shock. I could tell that something was drastically wrong from her voice. Then she said we had to sit down and talk with the doctor right away about a problem with one of the babies.

The doctor performing the ultrasound reported that the baby's head circumference was growing at an abnormal rate, and when he looked into it further, he found that the baby had an acute case of hydrocephalus. When I heard the grim news, I was appalled. I couldn't believe it. Why us? That was the question that opened the floodgates to all the other, awful questions: Will our baby be all right? Will our baby be like other children? Will our baby live? It was all too terrible to face. Nothing had prepared us for this.

All the talk about the brain—about a pressure build-up and its effects—and then being told that Kim required an emergency caesarean section right now, because the problem was so severe, absolutely shattered me. Kim was booked into Greenoaks Private Hospital in Bankstown straight away.

I had experienced the miracle of Mitchell's birth and treasure it as an irreplaceable memory. Seeing that little miracle, something Kim and I had produced, for the first time, had an effect on me that is beyond my ability to recount. Mitchell went full term, and his homecoming was one of the great joys of our life. With the emergency caesarean, however, everything was completely different.

Kim was on the operating table and remained conscious through it all—the doctors had given her an epidural. I was by her side, gripping her hand. We were both so afraid of what the future might hold for our little baby. The medical staff put a screen up, so neither of us could see when they slid Jessica, our healthy first-born twin, out. Then Rachel popped out.

My thoughts had been racing: What would she look like? Would she be normal in spite of the pressure on her brain? As soon as the doctor held her up to view, my instinct was to check how big her head was. I was speechless: our little baby not only had hydrocephalus, she had a cleft lip and palate. For me, seeing this disfiguration was even more upsetting than hearing about the hydrocephalus. I had never before encountered such a thing. I had heard people talk about a hare lip, but I had never heard of a cleft lip. What was that? Was it caused by the hydrocephalus? I had never seen one before medical repair. In the clinical environment of the operating theatre, the sight chilled me.

I was stony-faced, rock-eyed, silent, trembling; I felt like I was on a knife-edge. But I knew that I had to keep myself in check somehow and use whatever strength I could muster to focus on giving Kim the comfort and support she needed.

Sometimes doctors can pick up problems like cleft palates and lips early through ultrasound, but in our case they had not. They had no idea either. I saw our surgeon's face; he was distraught. The cleft lip was a complete surprise to him, too. But, like so many other medical professionals, he had that special gift—the ability to think about the patient's needs and feelings first. His priority was to give us the support, comfort, advice and encouragement that we would need to help us get through the first few hours, days, weeks. Not an easy task. I felt completely empty, drained; my world in pieces.

Kim stayed in Greenoaks for two weeks, but Rachel was transferred to Camperdown Children's Hospital on 7 March. The staff at Camperdown sat down with us and explained the medical procedures that they would be carrying out over the next few months. A kind nurse told us about her own daughter who had also been born with a cleft lip, and then, to reassure us, she brought in some photos to show us how her little girl looked after all the surgery. This was indeed comforting as we were so uncertain and afraid and we had so many decisions to make and medical problems to learn about and come to terms with.

As Rachel's difficulties became more sickeningly apparent, anxiety was our constant companion, day and night. The one as yet unanswerable question always present: would Rachel be all right? We asked about possible complications with hydrocephalus, and our doctor explained it all to us, but he made sure we also knew that it was impossible to predict what would happen in any individual case.

'There's a fifty-fifty chance she will be okay,' he said. 'It is possible that she will be normal mentally and will remain unaffected by it. Actually, there is even some good news—we did catch it early, which is good. These things can linger on and produce brain damage.' So we had caught it early. That was one positive.

Hydrocephalus is fluid on the brain. There are left and right compartments (ventricles) to every human brain, but in Rachel's case there was no communication between the two sides, which meant that the spinal fluid was not releasing quickly enough from her brain into her spinal chord. Ultimately, this medical condition is similar to spina bifida. Fluid builds up in the brain and the sides of the brain expand whenever the fluid can't get away quickly enough. This then places pressure on the skull, which is soft and flexible.

To remedy the condition, the doctors put two shunts into Rachel's brain, one on the right side of her skull and one on the left, so that when the pressure built up, the shunts would take over and release the fluid. Two tubes, located under the skin, come from her head into her stomach. There the fluid drains away, and she passes it through her water. The doctors have left a coil of tubing that is long enough so that as she grows, the tubes simply unfold.

They also placed two openings just above her

forehead, so that they can continue to conduct flow studies of her brain from time to time. They insert dye into her brain through those openings, and the dye lets them see whether the shunts are working properly. Using ultrasound and flow studies, they can monitor what is going on.

Eventually, Rachel had seven operations in five months (and may yet have to have others as she gets older), and the doctors repaired the cleft lip and palate. Before that, though, I remember vainly trying to feed her, only to find food coming out of her nose and ears, because they are connected. A hole is a hole, after all.

The time around Rachel's birth was very tough for the whole family. Jessica was a completely healthy baby with all a baby's normal needs, and at home we still had our 11-month-old son, Mitchell, to look after, too. We were split between home and hospital as we chopped and changed shifts, backwards and forwards between the two places. I would spend a day at the hospital and sometimes an evening, and then Kim would stay other nights. It was a bad time because circumstances kept us apart when we desperately needed to be together and give each other strength to carry on. Fortunately Kim's grandmother and mother stayed with us for three months helping out.

But if we were doing it tough, it was easy to see that others were doing it much tougher. Whenever I went to the hospital, I walked through the wards, saw the other kids, and instantly knew that we were more fortunate than many others. In a hospital you see your lot very accurately and clearly. Young lives are lost there every day, and in the face of that stark reality—life shining, then extinguished—our situation actually looked quite good.

Rachel was in the neonatal ward, which was full of little babies all looking so helpless. She was only a couple of weeks old and having operation after operation, so every day brought a new round of anxiety and worry. One afternoon, we had an appointment to see yet another report from Rachel's doctor on her progress—this time information on her stimuli response and motor skills. It stated that our little Rachel was unresponsive to any sound. Something was seriously awry with her hearing. Her specialist, Professor Gibson, found that she was deaf—even at 120 decibels (the level of noise a jet aeroplane makes). Rachel was eventually diagnosed as clinically deaf: just one more pain to add to a growing pile. My emotions went haywire. I felt I was losing it.

* * * * *

I had taken up a position with Crown Lodge, which belongs to Jack and Bob Ingham (brothers who made their fortunes in chicken farming and are now also very involved in racing), to become their stable jockey. This was a major move for us. We left the Eastern Suburbs and moved to Milperra.

Overnight I had become a man with an overload of commitments. I was still working—riding and trying to waste and keep my job—but with the medical procedures continuing, the pressure to stay on top of everything was almost unbearable, and I was not managing it at all.

Towards the end of the 1991 Autumn Racing Carnival period, while Rachel was still in hospital and having operations, I was really struggling with my riding because I felt overburdened. I had too much on my mind.

In racing you have to be focused on racing all the time. Every move you make on the track is crucial: you can endanger lives—including your own—if, in the midst of hard competition, your feelings are confused or you lack focus. This is what later happened to me in Hong Kong. Racing is a great sport, but there are risks. Because I lacked clear direction at this time, I was not succeeding with my rides.

Only days after finding out about Rachel's deafness, I was to ride at Royal Randwick Racecourse in the Adrian Knox 2000-metre race for fillies. The Knox is a lead-up to the Oaks, and a really important race, and that day I was riding a beautiful horse called Seasoning.

At the 700-metre mark, I was running sixth, two off the rails, and I moved out from behind another horse because Seasoning had difficulty accelerating. As I thrust out, instead of pulling or steering her, I tried to manoeuvre my body weight to push her out more quickly, but as I did, Grant Cooksley came up behind me. My elbow caught his elbow and matched him. It was not a deliberate move (although when I realised he was there, I did try to hold him out—after all, I was out there first). But as Grant rushed straight up, he brushed me, and our elbows hooked. Grant is known as 'the iceman'; he is one of the toughest competitors on the course, and he certainly was not going to budge a centimetre for me. Unfortunately, it looked on the replay as if I was trying to elbow him out of the way, so I was given a two-month suspension from the stewards.

I couldn't stop myself wondering about what was happening in my life. Why was everything that had seemed so good now turning sour? I had just taken a new

LIGHT

job and now I had landed a two-month suspension, and I had no idea what the future held for my new child.

I had to keep riding to give us some financial stability, so I appealed against the suspension. The Australian Jockey Club (AJC) knocked me back, and I now realise that it was for a good reason. The suspension meant I was able to spend more time with Kim and the kids, and time with them was exactly what we all needed. I hadn't been able to hold racing and my family responsibilities together, so the suspension and the rejection of my appeal were really blessings in disguise.

* * * * *

During the months that we tracked to and from the hospital, we would pass the hospital chapel on the way. Every time I went past I felt there was something special, almost eerie, about the place. One day I said to Kim, 'Look, I don't know what it is, but every time I go past this chapel, I feel I need to go in there—it's as if I'm being drawn in.'

'Well, maybe we should go in,' she said. 'How can it hurt?'

At this stage of my life, while I had obviously heard people talking about God, I really didn't understand what God was all about. I knew that people cried out to God when they truly needed help—and we sure needed help. I believed in God, but I had no understanding of Him whatsoever.

When we entered the chapel, I felt a genuine sense of peace immediately. It was another world, and one that I did not know at all. It seemed to be a million miles away from the chaotic life I had been living. It was certainly a place where I could look at my problems clearly and put them into perspective. I discovered a new depth and clarity in myself, but I was unable to name it.

I dropped to my knees and said, 'God, I don't know who You are, but we need help. Please help us.' Together, Kim and I cried out to God—the only person in the universe who could really understand and help us. There were no lightning bolts, no thunder splintered the roof beams, but this visit was an event that left a lasting mark on my life.

Eight months later, Kim's cousin Natalie convinced us to go along to the Christian Life Centre at Waterloo to have the pastors pray for Rachel. What did I think when someone suggested that pastors should pray for our little girl? I was open to the idea simply because I misunderstood it. I had no concept of what prayer meant at all, or what its power could be. The notion of people praying for healing was far from my world, but the idea that God could help us made me think back to the day we had first entered the chapel at Camperdown Children's Hospital. We had asked God to help us then, and I wondered whether this was how He was going about it. The chapel church connection made sense to me, it seemed to fit. There was something right about it—perhaps God could be found in both places. So we went along.

Rachel was healthy and thriving by now. Her cleft lip had been repaired, but we knew that there were still lingering doubts about whether she would be intellectually handicapped or not. We wouldn't know about that until she started to crawl, so that particular black cloud was still hanging around on the horizon.

Professor Gibson had already told us Rachel was clinically deaf and would never, ever hear. In fact, he had been quite blunt—he told Kim that if Rachel ever heard anything, it would be a miracle. So we just went and prayed. We had nothing to lose.

The healing service took place on a Sunday morning. At the appropriate time, the pastors told us to bring Rachel to the front of the church, and they prayed for her and anointed her with oil. There were four or five of them, including Pastor Frank Houston. We were all praying together, but I found it terrifying. Kim and I were standing before a crowd of total strangers—probably 800 or 900 people. I felt really embarrassed, unveiled; I could not hide. And they may have known who I was—by my guess there had to be a few punters there in a group that size. We stood there and let them pray for us, and I really expected nothing to come of it.

Some of the pastors were speaking in strange foreign tongues, which sounded like nothing I had ever heard before—the languages of heaven itself, I was to find out later—and I was thinking that I'd come to loopy land. What was this all about? This was crazy! (The New Testament Acts, written by a Greek doctor named St Luke, speaks about the gift of tongues, of men and women speaking in unlearned languages.) Speaking in tongues was too full on for me, too far from my world.

In the end I just accepted everything that happened during the service that day, and never deeply questioned it. After all, I was there mostly because I didn't want to be left out and I felt that Kim and I should be going together. So, when the pastors asked for people to give their hearts and souls to Jesus of Nazareth, I didn't take it too seriously.

I went forward to pray—but with my head, not my heart.

But, Kim gave her heart to the Lord, in absolute truth and sincerity, that day. She truly experienced Jesus. Unlike me, Kim made a heart commitment about her life and her future. On that day in May 1992, the day she wholly gave herself in faith.

A few days later, we went back to Professor Gibson and asked him to run more tests on Rachel. He did, and his report floored us. Her hearing had improved from complete unresponsiveness to a response at 90 decibels in her left ear and 95 in her right. She was not clinically deaf, but hearing impaired. Professor Gibson was unable to explain the change, and we were stunned—our prayers had been answered! We told him that we had been praying for God to help Rachel and that obviously God had come through. God had helped us. This was our first real sign that God can perform miracles in a life.

*****

Kim's life changed radically between 1991 and 1993—real, tangible changes. I could see them happening, and was unnerved by it all. Though we didn't go back to the Christian Life Centre until 1994, nearly three years later, Kim's personality and lifestyle were being transformed anyway, seemingly with no interference or influence from the church or pastors. God's Holy Spirit was already working in her life. And Hong Kong had certainly given the Holy Spirit every opportunity; the intensity of the hearings there and my eventual disqualification were like a pressure-cooker for her soul. Throughout these events Kim just grew and grew as a person.

When we returned to Australia, I was shattered. I was at rock bottom, dwelling in a black pit. Kim's support at this time was absolute and unwavering. She carried me. She was now mature and strong in her faith, and constantly seeking God. Her faith helped her find something extra to share with me and her strength and wisdom kept me going and pulled me through.

Soon after we returned, she asked me, 'Why don't we go back to the Christian Life Centre?' I hated the idea. My ban had been in force for two months, and while our marriage was slowly improving, things were still strained. My life was over, as far as I could see. In fact, my thoughts had become suicidal. I was spending most of my time alone, since most of the friends I trusted were in racing and I was not permitted to consort with anyone in the industry. Some days, I wandered around the cliffs of the Eastern Suburbs just looking for a crack so that I could slip or slide into it. I was depressed, had no self esteem and saw myself as a piece of dirt out of place in a clean room.

I told Kim that I was unwilling to go back to the Christian Life Centre because they were a bunch a loonies. 'Fine,' she replied. 'Then let's go to back to the Anglican Church where we were married, near Bondi Junction.' I agreed, and I fully intended to go along there. It was now February 1994.

But over the next few days, somehow something snapped, I found myself thinking about the Christian Life Centre and being drawn to go back there—the place where God, we believed, had healed our child. So we attended the services there for a few weeks. One Sunday morning the pastor was preaching up a storm, and while I remember little of his message, everything he said hit home. His arrows seemed to be aimed at me personally. The preacher was looking straight at me when he said, 'You can't do it on your own!' How did he know? That was exactly how I felt—that I was trying to do everything alone: beat the charges in Hong Kong, win races, take care of my family. That sentence did it: 'You can't do it on your own!' I fell back in my chair.

My mind was in a whirl. A niggling thought popped into my head and said it was a complete fit up, that Kim had told them how I was feeling. 'She's trying to change me and she has told the preacher, and now he is getting at me. Just wait until we get outside,' I muttered to myself under my breath.

Suddenly I felt something happening inside me, as if some kind of spiritual work was going on. My stomach was sure churning. My head and heart felt as though they were being turned inside out. Somehow I felt I was being challenged to really think for the first time about my principles, my outlook. I felt as though God was questioning me—that He had me under the microscope.

I heard the pastor ask people to make a commitment to Christ. I didn't have a clue what on earth that meant. What did it mean to have Jesus Christ as your Lord and Saviour? (Now I understand: it means to let Him be the great trainer, to take your place as an apprentice to Him.) Inside me it was a tug-of-war; should I go out or stay in my seat? Should I hold the reins tight and stay nice and anonymous or let go and stretch forward, be open, be seen? The urge to hold back was powerful; it felt pretty much like a heavy, wet track. But the call to come forward was clear—something even more powerful was pushing me to the front. I made a decision.

In full view of everyone, I got up out of my seat and took a step forward.

Neil Armstrong once said: 'One small step for a man, one giant leap for mankind.' Faith is like that. Stepping out in faith changed my life. I made a 180-degree turn and walked away from what I had been, to embrace something new. I reached the front of the church and simply broke down and cried. I knew that would happen because I had seen it happen to others. And I knew, too, that it would change my life forever.

It had taken 18 months for the penny to drop. Those hard times in Hong Kong, the pressure of the hearings, the shock of the disqualification, marriage troubles, then the loneliness, depression and self pity when I got back to Australia all set me up for the greatest confrontation of my life. By the time I got to the front of the church, I broke down. I repented. I brought my sins out in the open and owned up to who I truly was—not a bad guy, but not a good one either. Not as good a husband and father as I could have been. In fact I had been selfish, wilful and stubborn for years—all the things I loathed in a bad horse. And as I acknowledged all this publicly, I felt a great weight drop from my shoulders. I felt like a small child. No longer the great jockey, the hero, the Melbourne Cup winner; just a small person standing before God. And I was crying, too, in front of a crowd of people I didn't know, but who probably knew me. It was a humiliating experience, but it was tremendously freeing, too.

A strange sensation came over me taking me back to childhood. When I was six I called this feeling 'the monster', but it was a friendly monster, it always made me feel warm, safe, and protected. I never saw it; but I felt cocooned by it. Then I heard a voice deep inside me but just as clear as any human voice, 'I was with you when you were a child and I am with you now.' It was the Holy Spirit.

As I owned up to God about my sins and what I had done, who I had been, I knew I was forgiven. I said sorry from my heart; and I was genuinely sorry. I had missed out on what really mattered, yet now I experienced awesome forgiveness. I had carried around so much guilt, knowing that I had failed so often. I had let my family down; I had let God down. All this hung like a dead weight around my neck; I was unable to release the load.

But no sooner had I owned up to God than I was free. He let me go free of charge—no suspension, no appeals. Just complete and holy forgiveness. All the times I had said sorry to my wife or to my family for the way I was were irrelevant—the day I said sorry to God was the day real freedom entered my life. That day I experienced God's love.

I thought I knew how to love people, but when I encountered God, I truly discovered what love was all about. When you experience God's love, you realise that there is nothing else like it. You learn how to love others when you first give yourself to God.

As I stood meekly before God, the Holy Spirit told me to go home and to read Matthew 7:24: 'That verse is for you and concerns your life.' Kim had often read the Scriptures to let me know what God was like, but I had mostly ignored her; I thought she was a little off the planet. And when I had tried to understand what she meant, I had never grasped it. That night, though, when I came home, I picked up a Bible myself, for the first time. I was 28 years old.

I looked at that verse and it really was about my life: 'Anyone who hears these words of mine and obeys them is like a wise man who builds his house on the rock.' Because my life had been built on shifting sands, there had been no stability, no direction. Sure, I had success, but there had been no true solidity, no sure foundation. My life had been unstable, always moving around. The Scripture spoke about a man who listens to God—a wise man who builds his house on solid rock. As soon as I started to listen to those words, and be guided by them, my life became solid and sure.

* * * * *

Towards the end of my disqualification period, I asked the AJC to reduce the ban so that I could ride track work and get back into shape for racing. They got in touch with the Hong Kong Jockey Club, who agreed to a one-month reprieve so that I could regain my fitness.

The night before I was due to ride track work again at Randwick, I was sound asleep. Suddenly I was jolted awake at 3.30 in the morning—I felt as though a thousand volts of electricity was passing through me. My eyes were popping out of my head. Then the Holy Spirit spoke to me: 'Today, I want you to declare that you are a born-again Christian—not just a Christian, but a born-again Christian.' It was very specific. I was in shock; I wondered if I was hearing right. Then God's Holy Spirit said it to me again.

I got out of bed—I had to get to the track by 4.30—came downstairs and made a cup of coffee. Then I sat down and read the Bible. I asked God, 'What is going on?'

And then God spoke again: 'I am going to use you as an instrument for me in this world.' God was asking me to serve Him.

When I arrived at the track, there were enormous numbers of press there—radio, television, and print journalists, many more than I had ever seen before. I was taken completely by surprise. Some of the old trainers said they had not seen so much press at Randwick since the days of Tulloch, the champion Australian horse of the 1950s and 1960s. Everyone was asking for interviews, wanting to get the first grab. I asked them all to wait, so that I could enjoy the morning at the track first. And I did thoroughly enjoy it—there is nothing like those early hours, with the air scented with fresh, hoof-chewed turf and sweat-lathered horses. It was soothing to go back to something so familiar and so important to me.

When I had finished up, we held a press conference. The first question was a complete Dorothy Dixer: 'What was the greatest thing that happened to me during the nine-month ban?' The door swung wide open for me, so I plainly nailed my colours to the mast: I declared that I was a born-again Christian.

Media eyes boggled. 'What?' they shrieked. 'You're a what? A born-again Christian? What on earth are you going on about?' It was all too far from left field for them. 'What do you mean a born-again Christian?'

'Jesus is the Lord and Saviour of my life and I have become a Christian; I'm a believer in Christ,' I said.

The next day there were headlines everywhere; the story really hit. Christianity in racing was proclaimed that day. But I only did it because God asked me to. When God speaks, you do what He says. There is nothing to argue about; you are obedient. And that concept took the racing world by storm.

* * * * *

A huge crowd had gathered for my first race meeting after the ban. Everyone was expecting me to win because I was on one of Bart Cummings' horses. But I failed. I did not win until the following week at Warwick Farm, riding for Graham Begg. Then things started to happen.

A month later, I had my first group 1 win, on a horse called Navy Seal. Only God could have orchestrated this. I had been due to ride the favourite, Poetic King, but he had been scratched from the race. Navy Seal was 33-to-1, a rank outsider—a complete nag, I assumed. When I checked his form, it came up blank. Just goose egg after goose egg. This horse was a born loser. But I had no other ride, so I took it.

When I first saw the horse, I thought I must have been mistaken—he was just a pony compared with the others. I had a 51-kilogram weight to carry, but I wasn't concerned, because I didn't believe we would get a run; another horse would have to be pulled from the race before we would get a ride. But on the morning of the race another horse did pull out—a late scratching—so I was in.

The race was a shocker. I was three and four deep the whole way, but the horse got up and won anyway. That day I publicly gave thanks to the Lord. I remember little of what I said except that I gave the honour to God for what had happened in my life.

That year continued to be full of miracles. I was

given rides I should never have had, won more races than I ever had before, and eventually broke Billy Cook's 55-year-old record for the most winners in the city: I rode 128 that season, and Billy Cook's record was about 124 winners (pony races included). The whole year was just miracle upon miracle.

Poetic King also played his part in another strange event that year. When I returned to Hong Kong for the first time after my disqualification, I got a ride on Monopolise—the winning horse, as it turned out—after Poetic King was again scratched. I wasn't due to ride, but Poetic King cut his foot on a beach, so I took the ride and won.

From that day on, every time I had an opportunity to thank God and give Him the honour, I did. When I first started doing this, a couple of the trainers told me to cut it out—they said they had heard it too many times and were sick of it. One asked, 'When are you going to stop thanking God?'

'Mate,' I replied, 'you're going to have to get used to it, because I'm going to keep doing it. While I have breath in my body, I'm going to keep praising the Lord.'

And so I have. My life has not been an accident, yet if the Lord had not intervened in it, I can guarantee that today it would be less than it is. Like St Paul, I have had my Damascus Road and seen the light, and like St Paul I have to be honest about it. Anyone who truly knows me would expect no less.

3

CHILD

*To teach the inexperienced the ropes
and give our young people a grasp on reality.*

PROVERBS 1 (THE MESSAGE TRANSLATION)

CHILD

It's hard to describe 'the monster', but it was a warm, clammy, protective presence which came and covered me like a cocoon or a shell when I needed it, and gave me a sense of being invincible any time I was afraid. I had no idea what the monster was. But it was a very friendly monster and it simply arrived one day when I was aged six and stayed around until I was about eleven. After that, I didn't ever feel its presence again until I was a grown man of 28—that was the day I stood up and gave my life to Jesus Christ.

When I was very young, the monster appeared whether I summoned it or not, but when I realised the comfort it gave me, I began to call on it whenever I felt threatened. It was there in an instant, and made me feel safe, secure, and out of harm's way. 'The monster' was my way of describing the feeling it gave me—a deep sense of being protected, as if something big and powerful was standing right beside me. The monster turned out to be God's protection for a little boy growing up in the ACT.

* * * * *

On 17 November 1965, proud parents John and Robyn Beadman experienced the joy of birth for the first time: their baby boy arrived. They named him Darren John Beadman and he spent his first few days on the planet in Canberra Hospital with his Mum. His younger sister, Belinda, arrived 18 months later, and the Beadmans became a nice, neat family of four living in Garran, a relatively new suburb of Canberra.

We were a typical working class family: Dad was a plasterer and Mum worked a cash register at the local supermarket. Some of my earliest memories are of Dad telling me that he was always a hard worker, doing his best for the family. When he was younger, he had ridden horses and had even done some track work at Acton racecourse in Canberra. He loved horses with a passion, and because Mum was raised on a farm in Cathcart, she was also at home with animals (although she seemed a little afraid of horses and ponies at times). When I was three, Mum and Dad both agreed that it would be good for Belinda and me to work with horses from this early age.

We named our first family pony Trojan after the famous wooden horse used by the Greeks to conquer Troy. The Trojan horse had won the war for the Greeks and helped them recover Helen, wife of Menelaus king of Lacedaemon. Our Trojan's pedigree was not quite so grand; he was merely a willing little Shetland pony. Belinda and I learned to ride on Trojan under Dad's watchful tutelage.

Almost every weekend our family was on the road following the local show riding circuit in the districts around Canberra. Sometimes this meant travelling to places four hours away. We spent a lot of time together, which made us a very close knit family.

Trojan was kept on a property near Red Hill, just 15 minutes from home. We drove the family car, an old Morris Minor, to get out and back to see him. I learned to drive in that car on the property when I was just about seven, but as it turned out, I proved to be a better apprentice jockey than learner driver. One day, I lost control of the car on the dirt road approach to the property and smashed into its gate. The Morris Minor ripped the gate completely from its hinges. Needless to say, Dad was not pleased, and it was quite some time before I was allowed to drive the car again!

Spending time on the property with Trojan was Belinda's and my passion. As ponies go, Trojan was a true character—like the horse he was a named after, he was full of treachery. He was a rogue, with a poker face and a great bluffer. When Mum took us out to feed him, he knew he was on a good thing; she was edgy around him, and he knew exactly how much he could get away with. He had Belinda and me bluffed, plenty of times, too. Sometimes he chased us until we swung up into the branches of a tree, and would keep us pinned there until it suited him to let us down. But it was a different kettle of fish when Dad was around: then he was meek, mild and placid. I learned from Trojan that all horses have a mind and will that belong only to them. They are all unique personalities—no different from humans.

Although I loved riding, I had several other sporting passions as a child. We regularly attended rodeos, where I went in for potty-calf rides. Potty calves are about 10 months old and are the equivalent of a steer ride for a teenager or a bull ride for an adult. Children ride potty calves with ten-gallon hats, spurs and chaps—the full regalia. I even had my own calf rope!

The organisers, usually three grown men, would strap your hands down to the calf as hard as they could (in potty-calf riding you are allowed to hold on with both hands), place you in the shoot for ten seconds to get steady, and then let you go. A calf has loose skin, so your rope would inevitably slip a little, and the calf's vigorous shaking and twisting made it slice into your hands. It is only for the bold. At Moss Vale rodeo I once got hung up when my hands would not release from the rope, and the calf kicked me from pillar to post.

Potty-calf rides—of which I won a few in my time—were just a small part of the thrills and excitement of growing up around animals. Every kid loves danger, and a lifestyle full of horse riding and potty calves offered plenty of opportunities for that!

Outside riding, football was my other true passion, and I was a mean football player in my younger days. I played junior rugby union with the Magpies, a local team, and then I ventured on to rugby league with the Woden Valley Rams. Things were tough for me on the playing fields because I was a tiny squirt of a kid—definitely the runt of the litter. Nevertheless, I learned to hold my head high and to compete aggressively against bigger kids. I represented the ACT under 10s in rugby union, which, though not Super 12 calibre, was a big achievement for a small kid—perhaps it was a portent of bigger things for my sporting future? If I hadn't been a jockey, maybe I would have played for the ACT Brumbies? My uncle, Gary

Beadman, represented the ACT and Dad had been a good footballer, too. Those contests were great training—they toughened me for my years of riding at the top.

Between rugby and riding, there were few spare weekends; I never seemed to be at a loose end as kids are today. But I do remember one particular weekend when I was free. To this day I am unable to explain why, but a feeling came over me and I said to Mum and Dad, 'I want to go to a scripture class on Sunday.' Neither of them encouraged me to go, but nor did they stand in my way, so off I went.

I remember little of that class, but the urge to go sticks in my memory. Why did I want to go? Why did I think I needed it? Was God speaking to me even then? I never went to the scripture class after that: our family lifestyle—constantly travelling to riding venues—made it impossible.

I had a happy childhood, and my family was full of love, but there was a complete absence of any form of religion in our household. I had no idea what Christianity was or how it ticked until I was 28 years old and standing at the front of Sydney Christian Life Centre.

* * * * *

We were rarely involved in pony club activities; we mainly stuck to show events. Two factors combined to keep us from riding pony club: we lacked a suitable horse float to transport our ponies (by this time, Dad had built stables in our backyard because I now had my own pony, called Ben), and the nearest pony club grounds were five kilometres from home. The stables meant that we could keep our ponies at home. On the odd occasion we went to pony club events, Dad would walk us there on foot while Mum drove behind. We must have looked like a band of gypsies—two kids riding ponies led by a man walking and followed by a woman in a car! When we arrived at the turn-off to the pony club, Dad let us go on our own so that Belinda and I could gain the experience of mastering a pony by ourselves.

Ben, my pony, was a robust, energetic beast. The first time Dad let him loose, he bolted down the road faster than I had ever travelled. I was too small to control Ben or rein him in, so I just clung to him with all the strength I had. I had never felt the air whistling past at that speed. God seems to have blessed horses with instinctive knowledge about how to get rid of any nuisance on their backs. Somewhere, long ago, a very smart horse turned this instinct into a fine art by inventing the run-under-a-low-branch routine. Horses have passed this sacred knowledge down from generation to generation, and Ben had clearly inherited it. That day he ran me under dozens of low-hanging, scraping branches, but I lay low, flat, and parallel to his back with my head tucked in behind the nape of his neck, and he couldn't throw me. I beat Ben that day because I didn't fall off. It was my first experience of genuine speed, and while it was frightening, it was absolutely exhilarating.

Doing anything at speed involves that mysterious human hormone, adrenalin. The combination of speed and adrenalin have manufactured a rich array of human pursuits; whether it's cars, motorcycles, aeroplanes, boats or horses, the thrill of speed beckons to some reckless desire in all of us. That first taste of real speed, when I was only eight, intoxicated me.

Not very long after that, Dad took me to see a friend of his, a fellow called Mick Gavin. In his younger days, Mick had been a jockey, but now he was a trainer, and kept a few racehorses in his backyard. Dad and Mick sat me up on a racehorse, and I felt the amazing power of the beast below me as he stirred and skittered in the chill country air. Mick told me about jockeys, and said that with my size, I was a shoe-in to be a professional. Even at eight years of age, it was clear that I was a lot smaller than the average kid, and Mick could see that with training and development I could become a jockey.

After that day at Mick Gavin's place, the seed took root and I knew I was destined to be a jockey. I wanted that more than anything. I dreamed of it and nothing else from then on. As I continued riding the shows, I thought of the future—of riding for a living.

My grandfather, the late Ernie Beadman, watered the seed without knowing it. Pop was mad keen on racing, a fanatic, and every Friday and Saturday trots night he followed the form on his Golden Guide and showed me how he picked his tips. I learned all the jockeys' names and all the horses' names, and my dream began to take on some reality as I leaned about the racing world. It was such a well-known fact that I wanted to be a jockey that when I was 12 years old, the kids at school nicknamed me 'Jock'. At the beginning of November, before the Melbourne Cup, the other kids would start to ask, 'Which horse would you like to be riding, Jock?'

* * * * *

When I was ten, Mum and Dad bought a 40-acre (16 ha) hobby farm at Murrumbateman, a country town between Yass and Canberra, in the Southern Tablelands, and while they developed the property, Belinda and I stayed with my uncle, living in a caravan in his backyard for almost a year. I transferred to Lyneham Primary School in Canberra for that year. Finally, we moved out to the farm and lived on the land.

I absolutely loved it. Being able to invite my mates from school out, spend days with the horses and animals, camp out under the open skies, and do all the farmhand chores was a dream come true. Moving from the city suburbs to the country showed me another side of life—a side I have always loved. A wise man once said, 'You can take the boy out of the country, but you can't take the country out of the boy', and this has remained true for me throughout my life; while I love the comforts of living in the city, there is something about the country that always calls to me deep inside.

I was also working on the weekends for Hardwick Stud in Yass, run by the late Tony Freedman, father of the now-famous Freedman brothers. From the age of 11 onwards, I mucked out stalls, dressed horses, took horses to the gallops and cared for them. At Hardwick Stud, I was lucky enough to see how things worked in the engine room of the racing business.

Consequently, I knew the four Freedman brothers very well. In fact, we caught the same bus to school every day. They went to the local private school, while I was at the public school. The Freedman brothers were always on the bus before me and they regularly beat me up and gave me a hard time. But I got my own back. I competed against them in the shows, and while they always had the best horses and equipment, I let my riding do the talking. I used to beat them easily. They may have now conveniently forgotten this fact!

We moved to Moss Vale, in the Southern Highlands, when I was 14, and my association with Hardwick Stud ended. Now I worked for Mr Roberts at Burradoo, a small town between Moss Vale and Bowral. Any weekend that I was not riding in shows, I got onto my purple Malvern Star dragster bike and headed along the road to Burradoo. It was a good 5-kilometre ride. It took me about half an hour—and I went no matter what. And as anyone who has visited the Southern Highlands knows, it can be freezing cold in the mornings. But I would go anyway, cycling along the side of the dark road with no lights on my bike. I was happy just mucking out stables; I would do anything just to be a part of working with racehorses. That's how big my dream was.

My riding experience up till then had been with ponies, but at the Freedmans' Hardwick Stud and now, working for Mr Roberts, I learned to work with racehorses. Some of the horses were upwards of 18 hands in height, so they loomed huge and powerful out of the stalls. At my height, weight and size, it was a breathtaking experience to be so close to such size, and such relaxed strength. Racehorses have lean, sinuous, sculptured muscles, and when you work closely with them, you soon realise what awesome creatures they are.

It was while I was working at Burradoo, that I got to know Meg Iredale. She owned the sire of the pony I rode, and was a horse trainer herself. Meg lived at Moss Vale and trained her horses there, but she took the horses for fast work to Bong Bong, on the outskirts of Bowral. Bong Bong is an unusual 1400-metre track—it has a big hill in the middle—and was the location of the locals' picnic race meetings.

One day Meg asked me if I would like to come out to Bong Bong and ride a gallop. Of course I jumped at the chance, so off I went, to have my first ride on a genuine racehorse. I travelled a slow circuit first, with another jockey, Shane Butler, to hunt off all the dairy cows that made their mid-week home on the track. I looked like a pimple on a pumpkin on top of this racehorse, but I wound him up and had a good gallop.

A Bowral journalist was there and took a photograph of me, and that photo appeared in the local newspaper. I still treasure that photo, because that first run made me eager for many, many more; it lit the flame in me to ride the gallopers. My dream was taking a more definite shape.

Our life in Moss Vale was school, then afternoon chores, and riding. For Belinda and me, the work focused on our ponies. Every morning, afternoon and evening we took care of them, and we learned how to be totally responsible for something. The pony I had now was called Bilbo Baggins, after Tolkien's famous halfling in the book *The Hobbit*.

There is an old trotting track in Moss Vale called Lackey Park. It was around 20 minutes' ride from our house. By this stage, of course, Dad didn't need to help us with our ponies; we could saddle them up and ride by ourselves. So every day I saddled Bilbo Baggins, pulled the irons short, trotted him over to Lackey Park, and pretended to be trainer, jockey, race caller and owner, all in one. I ran my own race days at Lackey Park—and whenever I thought about racing, I thought about the Melbourne Cup, so I won the Melbourne Cup there so many times I should be the greatest jockey in history!

I galloped Bilbo Baggins day after day, and as I did, I would call the race: 'And here comes Darren Beadman down the outside…' And boy, could I come down the outside! Of course, I always won—pretty easy when you are the jockey, the race caller, and the stewards. (Looking back, I never had reason to call myself before the stewards.) As a consequence of all this work, my little pony was the fittest in Moss Vale—so fit that he possibly could have run in the Melbourne Cup! My dream was well and truly alive.

In Moss Vale I also began to realise how close I was to the animals, how much I understood them. I had very few friends; there were not a lot of other kids around to play with, so animals became my truest companions. If I ever had a problem, I went to talk to my pony. And if necessary, if the problem seemed insurmountable, I just cried on the pony's neck. That was all the comfort I needed. I shared my problems with the animals, and I suppose that explains much about my life and my career. I have always felt very at home with horses, always had an affinity for them, and a real understanding of them.

All horses have their own personalities. If you are patient and persistent, you will learn how to get the most out of them. Good horse people never break a horse's spirit because they know that once that happens, they lose the animal. As with humans, if an animal's spirit suffers defeat, the animal becomes crippled inside.

I learnt that horses need to have a lot of confidence

in the people who work with them. They gain that confidence through real, mutual experience, and when they see that you pose them no threat, they will work with you. Of course, some horses are cranky—they possess a difficult will that ill disposes them to people. But most horses, like humans, respond well to kindness and TLC. They want a tranquil life, just as we humans do, and they are prepared to work at relationships. Once a horse has confidence in you, and knows that you are not going to hurt it, but rather will support it, then you have a friend for life. You can call that horse in a paddock and it will come to you because it knows your voice and trusts the bond between you.

All in all, my early teenage years were simple and enjoyable. I was naive and unaffected by the temptations that seem to plague adolescent life these days. I wish I could say for sure why that was—maybe it was good luck, good judgement, fear of Mum and Dad, or the amount of time I spent with the horses. Perhaps it was all of those things, but I suspect now that it was God who kept me far from trouble.

The worst vice I ever tried in my life was smoking. Towards the end of my school days, I went away on a school camp, and some of the lads thought it would be great to buy some cigarettes. We bought them, took them down to the river, and smoked them. I only invested in six, but those six made me sicker than can be imagined. So I never smoked again, and there my wild teenage revelry began and ended.

By now I was nearing 15, and I no longer sensed the monster's presence. But I didn't need him, either, because I had become a confident young horseman, ready to tackle the world on my own. My life was moving on nicely. I had my dream, my passion; all I needed was a plan. How was I going to achieve my dream? How was everything going to fall neatly into place? I didn't have to worry for long, quite by chance the door opened. I met Sharon Hasler.

The year was 1980. Sharon used to take her kids around the shows for riding events, just as my parents did. We were standing at the Nowra Show talking about horses and racing. In those days, the most lauded New South Wales' jockey was Malcolm Johnston. His name was on everyone's lips because he was hugely successful. He had been trained by the most famous jockey trainer of them all—Theo Green. Naturally, I told Sharon that I wanted to be a jockey like Ron Quinton and Malcolm Johnston. Then she asked me who my favourite trainer was. I never batted an eyelid. She hardly had the words out before I blurted, 'Theo Green'.

To my amazement (and secret delight) she said that she knew him, and added, 'Well, I'll try to arrange for you to meet him.'

My eyes must have popped out of my head. What luck! True to her word, Sharon set it all up. She arranged a meeting for me through her father. It was to take place at High Street, Kensington, at the permanent stables of Theo Green, the great Sydney trainer, the man everybody in racing knew as 'The Boss'.

Mum, Dad and Belinda all came up to Sydney with me, and I made sure that I packed my famous photo—the one taken on the galloper at Bong Bong—triple-checking I had it on me before I got into the car. That precious photo would act as my Curriculum Vitae for a job application in the lightning-fast world of professional racing. My dream was about to come true: I was going to be a jockey, apprenticed to the sorcerer of the jockeys' trade in New South Wales' racing—Theo Green.

4

APPRENTICE

*On the fields of friendly strife
are sown the seeds that on other fields,
on other days,
will bear the fruits of victory.*

General Douglas MacArthur,
Inscription at West Point Military Academy

APPRENTICE

Perfection remains a human impossibility, but practice, dedication, commitment, and a liberal smattering of trial and error will develop the champion in all of us. Peak performance can be elusive, but all champions improve through learning from a master. Being apprenticed to a master led Michelangelo to greatness. Being apprenticed to Theo Green—the Boss— would lead me to the top of my profession. Without the Boss, I would never have achieved the success I did in racing.

The Boss knew how to get the best from young jockeys, and for all his apprentices—including me—he was happy to play the role of surrogate father.

My first impression of the Boss was of a tiny, jockey-sized man around 143 centimetres (4 feet 9 inches), in his mid-fifties, peering out at me through bright eyes buried deep in papery olive skin. The Boss had ridden as a young man, and it had been common, particularly in his younger days, for him to ride when training apprentices. But I never rode with him—he only trained for six years or so more after I began my apprenticeship.

His slight appearance was deceptive, because his voice was strong and loud, and boomed out from one end of his chaotic office to the other. The Boss was deaf in one ear, so you had to speak up. And when he talked, his voice had authority. You listened.

He commanded immediate respect. I was really nervous and shaking when I first stood before him in his stables. I quickly thrust out my hand and showed him the photo of me on the galloper at Bong Bong—my prized possession. He stared at it for a moment, with a quizzical look. His eyebrows furrowed (little did I know then how dry the Boss's sense of humour was), and he turned to me and commented, 'Well, I think we can do better than this, son.' He then proceeded to tear strips off my riding style as evidenced by the photo. I felt especially deflated when he dryly added, 'Now you see, son, your heels are too low. You're riding pony club style, and that's just not going to be good enough.' I suddenly felt as if I had never been near a horse before.

That interview experience shook me and I wondered what I was getting myself into—he offered me the opportunity to come and work for him and if I liked it he would apprentice me. I had started Year 10 at school and had to decide whether to finish the year or join the Boss at Randwick. Mum wanted me to stay at home, but Dad said the choice was mine. For me, there was no need to think about it for long—my passion and love for riding saw me quickly decide to leave school and join Theo Green at Randwick. It was 1981. I was 15.

I did not really understand at first what he was

saying about my riding style, but when I went to work as a stable hand at High Street, I started to note the subtle but all-important differences he was pointing out.

And what a shock the move proved to be! I was as green as a young tree. I was so wet behind the ears you could have washed with me! I took up my accommodation in Clear Day Lodge in High Street, Kensington, and my eyes were opened wide. I came from a nice, clean, family home. Now I found myself in a small bunkroom—three double bunks next to a shared toilet—and living with some pretty desperate characters. There were jockeys and strappers in the room, ranging in age from 15 to 30—this guaranteed that what I saw going on (drugs, women…you name it!) made me grow up fast.

I arrived in Sydney with no life experience whatsoever, $100 in my pocket, and a brown suitcase full of clothes clutched in a trembling hand. For the first few months, I literally lived out of that suitcase, because I couldn't unpack—there was no drawer to put my clothes in. With six of us in the room during the week, things always became uncomfortably cramped on weekends, when more young guys would come up to try their luck in professional racing; the Boss received applications week in, week out, and all those willing to try their luck ended up sleeping on the floor of the bunkroom.

The kid on the floor became the 'munchie boy'—it was his job, late at night, to get snack food for the older guys. It was an open-all-hours job; the munchie boy was woken up at anybody's whim and sent to the shop, no matter what the time, circumstances or prevailing weather conditions.

But I was no problem for the munchie boy, because I

avoided fatty foods. I restricted my diet to stay in shape, even though we constantly worked and burnt off whatever kilojoules we consumed. Every day began with track work, followed by exercises, mucking out stalls, caring for three horses, afternoon work and various other chores. It was a 15-hour working day, seven days a week, starting at 3.30 in the morning (5.30 on Sundays). We took floats to the races, strapped horses, and then worked at the stables until 5.30 in the afternoon. Then, after our one and only meal for the day, we struggled into bed at about 7.30 pm.

The sauna became our second home, since we all had to keep our weight down. If I had not continuously wasted and taken saunas, doctors told me, I would have grown to 70 kilograms and five foot nine—too big for a jockey. These were the sacrifices we had to make to stay in the business. But it was all worth it. I knew that I had a future and the Boss confirmed it.

The Boss often asked the press to come down and see his boys in action. That was his way of helping your career. I had not been with him long when *The Sun* newspaper's turf editor, Max Presnell, who still writes a column in Sydney, came down to Randwick to talk to the Boss. The article he wrote about me appeared in *The Sun* on Thursday, 9 July 1981:

> *Fifteen-year-old Darren Beadman is set to follow the trail blazed by leading jockey Ron Quinton.*
> *Even now Beadman is being compared to Quinton, although he is still a 'kindergarten' pupil with master teacher Theo Green.*
> *It would appear that the Green machine is*

about to produce another top rider but you will have to wait for Beadman—he won't appear in races for at least 12 months.

'Darren, in eight days, picked up what it took Ron Quinton eight months to learn…'

This was just one of the quotes from Theo Green, the master tutor of apprentice jockeys, about his latest protegé.

Although still in 'kindergarten' at the Green school, the teacher is tipping a big future for 15-year-old Darren Beadman.

If you haven't got a good memory, mark the name down, because Beadman, from Bowral, has joined the Green string and won't be apprenticed for another 12 months.

But the old master is already going into raptures about the teenager.

Now it is not unusual for Green to put a boom on one of his boys, but he rarely comes on so strong.

In the past he has had plenty of cause when you consider his previous graduates – Gordon Spinks, John Duggan, Ron Quinton, and Malcolm Johnston.

However he is already comparing this recent addition with his best…

'He has got something—it's difficult to explain. I just feel it,' Green explained.

'Look at him,' he said and passed his binoculars so I could observe Beadman riding a track gallop at Randwick last week.

He sat cool and was perfectly balanced.

> *Green compared him with Gordon Spinks—'He has the best seat on a horse of any boy I've had.'*
>
> *Considering his youth, the lad has a certain style and confidence, but I can't say he looks any better than Andrew Pettit, another student at the Green academy.*
>
> *'Take into consideration that Darren is just starting,' Green said.*

That was the Boss. I had done nothing to deserve such a glowing rap, but he knew what it took to get a jockey's career moving. Without media support, a jockey is nothing; they can make or break you. As a jockey, you are only as good as your last ride, and trainers and owners read the papers and watch television, too, so getting on well with the media is vital. The Boss knew that and was determined to give us the best go he could because he believed in us.

Not long afterwards, on 27 July 1981, he made another prediction about me. *The Daily Mirror* was doing a story on Andrew Pettit, Theo's new 16-year-old apprentice, and the article was glowing with praise about him and his trial rides. But the Boss commented, 'There's a better one at home.' The journalist, Tom Brassel, picked up on that remark, and the paper ran the story under the headline: 'Andrew Makes Grade...And there could be a better one at home.' He wrote, 'Theo makes no secret of the fact that he believes Darren Beadman, who is only 15, shows more natural ability than any of his previous champs displayed when they came to him.'

The Boss was always quick to give you a plug, and it

certainly helped my career along. Media coverage like that is priceless for a jockey's career, and I was not even apprenticed at this stage. From the very beginning, the Boss made sure that we knew how to keep ourselves sweet with the press. It was just another part of making sure your career would go well—he was just keeping the oven warm.

The Boss was a very strict man, but also very fair. He was committed to promoting his boys. While other trainers promoted their horses, concerned themselves with getting the best riders, and hardly bothered with apprentice jockeys at all; the Boss always took on apprentices, always promoted his boys, and let them race on his horses.

Theo is a mighty character, full of integrity. This was a crucial time in my life—when I was 15 and 16 years old—and I could have turned in many directions and perhaps have made poor choices, but he took on a fatherly role and kept me on the straight and narrow. He not only taught me to be a good jockey, but he gave me solid principles for life—respect, honour, courage, discipline, a hard day's work, and how to treat other people—and while I failed to live up to these on many occasions, I believe that his training has helped me to be better than I might otherwise have been.

These principles have stood fast in my life and, I believe, saved me when things fell apart in Hong Kong. If others had not marked me as a man of integrity, I doubt I could have come back into racing; and, to a large degree, I have the Boss to thank for that.

* * * * *

The Boss gave me my first race ride, too, on a horse called Royal Sheba at Rosehill Gardens. It was Wednesday, 2 June 1982, and the race was the Lilyfield Handicap, over 1400 metres. I thought I was home first, but a horse called Avon Time pipped me at the post. I wasn't too disappointed with second place, but it certainly would have been better to win!

Before that race, I had only ridden 24 barrier trials. (Barrier trials are trial races, without betting, and exist to train and mentally prepare horses and jockeys for race conditions. They give you an education about a race without being too competitive.) I would not have had such a great start if the Boss had not believed in me.

No better example of his faith in me was our win in the 1984 Golden Slipper. Coming in to the Slipper I had been racing a horse called Inspired. The Boss had trained him, educated him, and strapped him. Inspired was a highly-strung horse and was nervy around the barriers, but he had the heart of a champion. In the weeks before the Golden Slipper, I had won three major races on him. In the final week, we had to win the Pago Pago to qualify for the Slipper. There was plenty of pressure on the Boss because other jockeys—jockeys with better credentials than me—were ringing to get the ride, but he stuck with me, and the horse got home.

So we were through to the Slipper. The Boss again hung in with me, and gave me a chance in a major race, and the Slipper became ours. (Wayne Harris is the only other apprentice jockey (and the youngest—pipping me by a few months) to win the race.) Without the Boss keeping faith with me then, my career could have been stunted; the Slipper really thrust me into the limelight. The

Slipper paid $325,000 to the winner then, but today it is a $2 million race.

Loyalty is a two-way street, and I made sure I always kept faith with the Boss—I wanted to please him, and to show him how serious I was, so I worked hard. We all walked exercise in the afternoons, and he followed behind us. He would grill us all, talking to us and drumming in the lessons of the jockey's trade. He never seemed to run out of words of advice and encouragement. Going to the races, coming home from the races, he kept at us, pounding away like a cannon until we learnt the lessons. He was always asking questions, too: 'Now, son, why did you do that?' And you had to explain your moves, your style, what you had done and why.

Every morning, Theo worked us through physical drill and preparation. Even today, having been out of professional racing for 6 months, I have a neck size disproportionate to the size of my head because the Boss made us work our neck muscles; he had been a boxer in his youth and knew the sort of jarring the head can take. I believe that this practical piece of wisdom has saved my life, particularly in the bad falls in Hong Kong. The Boss believed that the most vital part of a jockey's anatomy is his neck—if you fall, invariably it is on your head. No kids at other stables had this kind of physical preparation— only the Boss's boys.

* * * * *

Life at High Street could be funny at times. My initiation into the jockey's world came in the form of a command from the older lads to go down to the garage to get some equipment because the horse I was riding in the morning would be handicapped and needed a heavy weight. The older boys reassured me that the bloke at the garage would know what I needed because he supplied these things all the time. 'Go down and ask for a long weight,' one of the guys said.

True to form for a green country kid, I trudged down to the garage and asked the guy behind the counter for a long weight. He looked at me strangely and left me standing there. I waited and I waited, but nothing happened. Finally, I began to get annoyed at the hold up; I wondered when he was going to get this weight. I suppose it shows how simple I was, but I waited ten minutes or so until the guy said, 'Mate, I think you've had your long wait! See you later—you can go now!' Then the penny dropped.

The older blokes got me on another occasion, too. They told me that the Boss had a right-handed whip, but because a particular horse hung in badly and needed to be motivated from the other side, someone had to get a left-handed whip. Of course, I fell for this too, and scurried off to the local supplier for a left-handed whip. The supplier pulled out two whips and asked, 'OK, which one's left and which one's right?' They'd stung me again!

* * * * *

Riding as an apprentice was breathtaking. I loved it. I won my first race at Wyong—the Wyong Handicap over 1350 metres—on 8 July 1982. The horse, Flagette, was a 20-to-1 outsider, trained by the late George Brown. Flagette kept a fast finisher, Wilkness, at bay to get home.

Not long after, I rode my first city winner—Gaelic

(at 6-to-1)—in the Leumeah Welter at Warwick Farm, but I nearly missed out on the ride altogether: I took a very bad fall at the 500-metre mark in an earlier race and they had me in a stretcher and heading for an ambulance until I managed to argue my way out and keep riding. Nothing had gone right that day until the last race, when I came home on Gaelic.

All in all, my apprenticeship was marvellous in terms of the wins I had. I was runner-up dux of apprentices once during my four years and leading apprentice twice. The other year I was away in France. Apprentice jockeys have an 'allowance' of 60 wins in the city for the period of their apprenticeship, and to begin with, they carry a weight of 3 kilograms. (After you complete your allowance, you have to compete with all the older jockeys on level terms, even though they may have 20 years of experience on you.) I out-rode my allowance in 15 months. A lot of apprentices never even reach their allowance.

By 1985, however, with one year of my apprenticeship remaining, I had begun to head into a drought—70 races without a winner! The Boss's instincts told him that I needed a change of scenery, and a chance presented itself when Paris-based Aussie trainer John Fellows invited me over to France to race. The Boss urged me to go. It was unusual for an apprentice to leave his or her master, but Theo saw advantages in it for me and encouraged me. So I packed my bags for France. I spent nine months in La Morlaye, near Chantilly, where Fellows kept a stable of about 90 horses.

Because I had not driven a car since my days of gate crashing in the family Morris Minor, and because I was going to France by myself, I told the Boss I needed to get a licence so I could get around in France. (The Boss permitted none of his boys to get a licence until near the end of their apprenticeship.) To my delight he said, 'That's right, son, you'll have to do that.' To this day I don't know how I got that one over him!

When I went to the RTA office at Rosebery, I stood at the counter and waited for someone to serve me. But people kept going past me to get help. Finally a guy caught my eye and said, 'What's up?'

I said, 'I'm here to get my licence.'

He smiled and said, 'Well, stand up.'

I replied, 'I am, mate!' With my baby face and small stature, people thought I was waiting for my mum. When I gave him my name, he clicked onto who I was, and in an urgent fluster he took me out for my test. He was totally uninterested in my driving (he failed to notice my botched three-point turn); he only wanted to know my tips for the weekend!

* * * * *

In France I rode 25 wins in about 200 races. I won the Prix Morny, the big two-year-old race—the French equivalent of the Golden Slipper—on a filly called Regal State. I rode all the major tracks. It was a different type of racing in France. Trainers gallop their horses in huge open forests and on sand tracks; in Australia, training methods are more modern—on racetracks in cities, running in circles.

France was a complete culture shock for me—I did not speak a word of the language when I arrived, and I went from living in a room with five other guys to having my own house in the French countryside. With the help of my French tutor I could manage pretty well by the time I left, but my initial lack of mastery of French made me the butt of many jokes and an easy target generally.

Here's an example. I was 19 and still pretty green when a French jockey named Maurice Phillipron abused me for riding through a gap—it was certainly a skinny run, but one that we would always take in Australia. He came into the jockeys' room cursing in French and calling me a stupid kangaroo and Skippy, so I left the room and went into the toilets. He came in after me with his towel wrapped around his neck. He closed the door, but I stood my ground. He glared at me, trying to bluff me, but I still didn't budge. He gave me a rev-up, threatened me, and told me that he was the kingpin and never to cross him. But he said it all in French.

I glared back at him and said, 'I know you speak English because I've heard you, so don't come in here yelling at me in French. If you've got something to say, say it in English.' He moved forward menacingly. 'If you're going to have a go, have a go,' I added. Maurice backed off. He was a grown man, stronger than I was, and he was just testing the water to see if he could control me. From that day on we actually became mates, and all the other guys gave me a healthy clearance.

* * * * *

Before I left for France I had met Kim in a nightclub. We were introduced through a friend. We talked and, trying to impress the socks off her, I told her that I was just buying a house. I quickly found out that Kim knew little about racing, but what she knew, she despised. She had grown up in a home where the form guide and the wireless coverage of racing were a given, part of the furniture. Racing definitely didn't appeal to her, so when I told her that I was a jockey, she seemed singularly unimpressed.

Kim was training to be a nurse, so she couldn't visit me in Kensington—I had to get over to Bondi to see her. My apprenticeship wages were only $68 a week, and most of that (whatever didn't go on race gear) then went on taxi fares to Bondi!

One day, early on in our relationship, I jumped a taxi to Kim's house and stopped on the way to grab some pantyhose and a paper. (Jockeys wear pantyhose under their silks to reduce the friction on their thighs.) When I got to Kim's place, a fit of nervousness suddenly gripped me: she was my first girlfriend, after all. I sat in her kitchen while she got ready to go out, and I stared around, whistling and looking at the ceiling. I put my pantyhose down on the table and read the form guide. Kim and I spent the afternoon together, and when I grabbed a taxi back to High Street, I left my pantyhose sitting on the kitchen table, where Kim discovered them. She rang me, and the conversation finally got around to my pantyhose. Needless to say, she was greatly relieved when I explained why jockeys use women's pantyhose.

I had only known Kim for six months when I had to pack my bags for France. Once there, I spent most of my earnings on phone calls back to her in Australia. I was so lonely, and we were falling heavily for each other.

Our relationship grew and developed long distance, but as it did, Kim felt under pressure to tell me about something she was sensitive about. As things became more serious, she began to sweat on telling me, wondering when the right time would be. After six months of phone calls from halfway across the world, she finally broke the news. She said, 'Things are getting serious, and I didn't know when to tell you or what to say...'

I gasped, because I thought the worst—she must have another boyfriend and it was all over. After all, it was a long distance relationship and I had been away for six months. However, I got up the pluck to ask, 'Well, what's wrong?' I dreaded the answer.

She blurted, 'I'm Aboriginal.'

I was unsure what to say. I had thought with her olive skin that she must be Greek or Italian. I had never met her family. I was shocked. It was as if someone had landed a surprise right hook. I had grown up in an Australian society where racial prejudice was pretty widespread. I didn't handle her news well at first. I didn't really know what to say. But then I thought: 'So what? I really love Kim. Who cares? So what if Kim is Aboriginal? What difference could it possibly make to us?' I could only answer with my heart, and my heart loved Kim and told me that race was irrelevant. Differences in nationality or race have nothing to do with who we are. After all, you marry a 'who', not a 'what'.

Kim and I got married in 1989 and we decided to tie the knot at St Mary's, a small Anglican church in Bondi Junction. It was such a happy day with our friends and family that if I had died right then I would have been in bliss. Today, I feel very grateful that through our marriage God has given us an opportunity to experience first-hand the national reconciliation that many in Australia yearn for. I feel proud to know that I made the right choice, even before I knew Christ, and that I had enough common sense to trust my heart. It sickens me to recall that I even wavered for a moment. I was not really a bigot, but I certainly gave the evil of prejudice a space in my mind for just an instant. If I had let that doubt grow, I would have missed out on Kim. I believe that God joining us together shows that there can be reconciliation between white and black.

* * * * *

    I would have gone back to France in 1986, but I was so homesick over there that I hesitated to return. The desire not to return became a firm decision when my sister, Belinda, had a tragic car crash that year. She was in Prince Henry Hospital in traction for eight weeks. Two of her neck vertebrae, the C6 and C7, turned to powder in the crash. I needed to remain in Australia to be near Belinda and my parents, so I stayed, and finished my apprenticeship with Theo Green in March 1986.

    My apprenticeship was a peaceful time. I never, ever copped a pay-out from the Boss because I was always diligent, and always did the right thing by him. There was one slight exception, though, which I am sure he still knows nothing of.

    When I got back from France, I used to go to Kim's house on a Saturday night. It was late, this particular night. We had been out for the evening and I was tired, so I fell asleep on Kim's couch. But the Boss did not allow his boys to sleep out—we had to be at the lodge every single night. Luckily, one of the lads knew where Kim lived, so the foreman, Kenny Stone, one of my dearest friends in the world, sent him to Kim's to find me before the Boss came to the track. I had never missed a morning's work in five years. I was there every day, without fail, at 3.30. Sunday morning was a luxury—we didn't have to start until 5.30. But at 5.30 that day I was still missing. Someone banged on Kim's door, and I almost jumped out of my skin.

'Quick,' he urged. 'The Boss isn't there yet, so if we hurry, we might just get you back in time.' We jumped in his car and scooted back. I still thank the Lord that the Boss was not there when we drove in to Randwick. Kenny did not bother to ask for any explanations; he just told me to go inside, get into my track work gear, and jump on a horse. And I did. If the Boss had caught me, he would have torn strips off me, even though I only had a few months to go in my apprenticeship—I was still under his care, and it was not the done thing. Besides, it set a bad example for the younger apprentices. In any event, I doubt the Boss ever discovered my one secret lapse as an apprentice!

* * * * *

Completing my apprenticeship was a lasting thrill. To master anything in life, particularly systematic training for 15 hours a day, seven days a week for four years, is a testimony to both student and teacher. It is an achievement that prepares you for the real job ahead.

A jockey's apprenticeship is four years long for a reason: to prepare tradespeople for the competitive world of professional racing. As preparation goes, I could have asked for no better role model or mentor than the Boss. He laid the foundations for my future success by instilling in me the discipline necessary for peak performance in the exacting world of racing.

The Boss never let up, never let you give or accept second best, and when I left my apprenticeship to go it alone, I finally understood why. Those four years got me ready to stand on my own two feet in what, in my opinion, is one of the greatest sports and most challenging industries that human beings have had the creativity to invent.

Apprentice jockeys keep none of their winnings—they go into a trust fund with the AJC until the apprenticeship ends. I had won over one hundred races, including the Golden Slipper, as an apprentice, so when my apprenticeship ended I had enough money to buy a house at Mascot and a car—and still have a bit left in the bank.

5

RACING

Do they know? At the turn to the straight
 Where the favourites fail,
And every atom of weight
 Is telling its tale
As some grim old stayer hard-pressed
 Runs true to his breed,
And with his head just in front of the rest
 Fights on to the lead…

A B 'Banjo' Paterson, Do They Know?

RACING

An apprenticeship in any field is a wonderful thing; it guarantees you a trade, a skill that you can turn into an income, if you are good enough. Coming out of my apprenticeship in 1986, however, I realised that my years in the Green academy were not going to be sufficient to get me to the top. I knew that I would have to work very hard, ride constantly, and be committed to doing the things others would not do, if I wanted to be successful. And I wanted that more than anything.

I started out as a freelance jockey, riding for any stable and choosing the mounts I wanted, but Bobbie Thomsen, another Randwick trainer, made me his stable jockey the year that I graduated and I worked for him for several years. The years between 1986–90 became something of a trial period for me, as I criss-crossed New South Wales, riding horses wherever and whenever I could. I was committed to improvement, so it mattered little to me whether I rode metropolitan races or country races—I just wanted to improve my skills.

And I did improve. I was doing the hard yards that others did not do, and that brought me success. I saw my ranking rise until I was listed in the top five in the land, but I never seemed to get any higher. So I just kept my nose down, kept pounding out the yards and plodding toward my goals and dreams. One particular dream was the Melbourne Cup, but I kept that in my back pocket, not knowing when I would get a chance on a serious contender. I kept growing and improving, living in hope of success.

If I thought that I was on a steep learning curve in racing, it was nothing compared with marriage. I simply had no idea about the commitment and responsibility required of me. I think there needs to be an apprenticeship for marriage, too! I was very young and immature and we had a family immediately. So our marriage suffered a lot in those days. I only felt comfortable racing horses. I felt inadequately equipped outside of that world, so I focused on what I knew how to do, and do well.

Because there was so much to learn in racing, I just kept my nose to the grindstone and went for it. I knew that if I kept going, I would find success. That was the period when I earned my stripes in racing. I won plenty of events, and I got to know key people, who would later influence my career. I marvelled at the industry I had entered—it had so much to teach me. I wanted to learn all I could. And I wanted to win. Winning the Melbourne Cup in 1990 really put me on the map of Australian racing, and it would also get me mixed up with every major player in the industry. Winning that race put me in the major league. It seemed Lady Luck was smiling on me.

RACING

* * * * *

Jockeys think constantly (some more than others, of course!). Every move must be anticipated many steps ahead. Time and distance must be united within a plan, and then juggled with the actual race, where sometimes nothing goes exactly to plan. It is a jockey's job to know that a move at the 1600-metre mark will lead to a certain position at the 800-metre mark. Because of this mental strain, jockeys tire mostly in the mind—very rarely in the limb.

Racing is, therefore, more mental than physical. There is a physical side to racing—you have to push the horse, lift the horse, and provoke the horse so that you get the best from it, particularly in the last 300 or 400 metres. Consequently, a ride is physically like a 400-metre sprint for humans, and you arrive at the post completely puffed out—you have sweated out your energy on balance, poise, and speed. If you race well, you will have expended great amounts of energy, and though you may not be winded like a 400-metre runner, you will probably have used up more mental and emotional energy. Your body does feel this, especially after eight events in the same day.

Jockeys expend this energy day after day. And they do so after gruelling hours of shedding weight in saunas. Mental exhaustion and fatigue are common, but owners and trainers expect jockeys to be as mentally and physically composed for the last race of the day as they were for their first ride. Riding looks easy, but it is strenuous. Put the average recreational rider in eight gruelling races in a day—and he or she would wilt under the stress. It is a specialised field and that is why the apprenticeship is so long.

Apprentice jockeys learn to work 15 hours a day, seven days a week, for one reason: to increase their ability to manage these levels of stress and effort. The hard work is like getting ready for a test; it sorts out those who will make the cut in professional racing and those who will not. Without the apprenticeship system, jockeys could not be properly prepared for the rigours that lie ahead.

Every move you make on the course is under the microscope. The stewards are watching with upwards of eight cameras; the owner needs to know that you did your best; the trainer wants to know if you are worth employing again; and punters need to know that you gave their money every chance to be multiplied. And you have to know how to handle that pressure.

Because of this stress, not every jockey rides at 100 per cent every day. Many jockeys have high highs and low lows; they peak and trough. They win for a while, then crash and burn. Then they come back again.

In my younger days, I fell into the peak and trough group, but deciding to aim for consistency got me to the top. This is another factor that separates the winners from the also-rans. I tried to ride at 90 per cent all the time, and for specific occasions like the Melbourne Cup, to lift myself to 110 per cent—to ride the unrideable ride. At 90 per cent I found a balance, found consistency. My 90 per cent got me through 90 per cent of the time. Consistency is one of the major keys to winning.

Because of the mental and physical pressure of racing, I often went home to bed after a long race day and found I could not sleep. I was exhausted—I ached for rest—but I was too tired for sleep. Once I did drop off, though, I found it hard to wake up. I would feel so flat that I would neglect a lot of sport outside of racing; all I ever wanted to do was to give my body a rest. When you ride 22 to 24 races a week, and morning track work, you end up exhausted. You ride 60 horses a week, so you have to always be fit to perform and win.

Racing is hazardous for precisely this reason. People die on racecourses because so many things can go wrong, and because it is physically impossible for jockeys to be aware of everything every moment. Human durability lasts only so long. And after durability is exhausted, there is only luck, pure and simple.

I have known jockeys who have set off alarms going through metal detectors at airports because they have so many nuts and bolts in them, courtesy of race falls. I was blessed in that way in my racing career—I had few falls and never damaged any major internal organs. My falls were never serious, except for Hong Kong, and even there, by some miracle, I suffered no major injuries. Others were not as lucky—I have seen people seriously injured on racecourses.

* * * * *

Racing in Australia began very early in the colony's history; Governor Phillip brought six horses of mixed breed to New South Wales on the First Fleet as work horses; but it wasn't long before thoroughbreds were being imported exclusively for racing. Racing flourished from the earliest days of the colony and today it is a multi-billion dollar industry.

While gaming is not exclusively an Australian

phenomenon, Australians do tend to have flocked to it as a leisure pastime in an unprecedented way. The old cliché that Australians will bet on two flies crawling up a wall does seem to be independently supported by statistics.

Supported by an enormous influx of capital through gambling (some $11.36 billion in 1996–7), generating enormous prize money, and offering outstanding personal and professional rewards, racing is now the third-largest industry in Australia. The number of people directly and indirectly employed in the industry is absolutely staggering. The turnover and money involved directly in the industry, plus the amount of revenue the government gleans through taxes, make this industry an important contributor to Australian economic life as well as to its social fabric.

And no matter what one may believe about the deleterious effects of gambling at the individual human level—and there certainly is ample evidence of its harmful effects—society also benefits from gambling through the taxes it raises: schools, hospitals, roads and community activities all receive some of this. In this sense, gambling on horses is a major contributor to Australian cultural, civic and economic life.

Government revenue from gambling in general far outweighs any contribution made specifically by racing (figures from 1996–7 show that lottery and machine revenue totalled $68.63 billion), but horseracing is nonetheless an astounding contributor. Australians seem to have a special affinity with this particular sport.

In general terms, if you are talking about 'the racing industry', you are talking about revenue, employment opportunities generated through the breeding industry—

those who own studs and retain stallions and mares—and the produce industry (those goods and services needed to maintain breeding). Horses need food (they may devour 4 or 5 kilograms of high-fibre grain and chaff every day, and chew through unlimited amounts of hay), transport, veterinary care, and equipment. And administration adds another level. This all contributes to the economy.

People who breed horses vary in their level of interest in the sport; some breed horses as a business and some do it as a hobby. The same is true in racing, where some people treat it as a business, and others treat it as a hobby. Everything depends upon the depth of commitment of the individual. In general terms, however, the industry appears to be on an upswing, with increasing activity and revenue.

Statistics tell us that there are 459 racing clubs in Australia, 401 racing venues, and 3274 race meetings annually. In total, in 1996-7 there were 22 935 races conducted in Australia, offering prize money of $256.43 million, with combined prize money in Victoria and NSW a staggering $154 million. Overall, there were 218 859 starters in races in 1996-7: 32 541 individual horses. By every measure, the industry is alive and well.

The Australian breeding industry has also become more important and accepted internationally. 'Shuttle' stallions (stallions who move from place to place to service mares) that formerly only bred in the Northern Hemisphere now also travel south, to breed here. There is a greater international flavour in Australian racing for precisely this reason. Australian racing tended, in the past, to do business only with New Zealand—the nearest racing arena in our time zone—but now the industry is global.

Most trainers (there are still some hobby trainers) treat the industry as a business, as do some owners. The majority of the owners probably treat the industry as more of a hobby, something of a toy, but there are some serious owners, such the Inghams, Robert (Bob) Lapointe and Nick Moraitis.

The Inghams, for example, now turn over about $10 million a year through their horseracing ventures, so they can hardly be called hobby-owners. Their business has only been going for around 14 years, and has grown enormously and rapidly in that time. Their Woodlands stud, for instance, which was first established as a property in 1824, covers 6000 acres (1200 ha) in the Hunter Valley. The Inghams may stand up to seven stallions at a time, but their champion is the Big O—my friend, Octagonal. A servicing by Octagonal can cost upwards of $30,000.

Most horses are owned by a syndicate, known as 'connections', and many connections see the industry as something of an investment. For example, a syndicate owns 1995 Melbourne Cup winner Doriemus. You will often find 'connections' sniffing around the yearling sales for a bargain (yearling sales take place around January to April each year).

New Zealand seems to produce more good horseflesh than Australia, but the Australian industry has the money, so more often than not, Australian owners will purchase in New Zealand for the Australian market. New Zealand has some horses of outstanding size—Phar Lap, obviously, and Sir Tristram, more recently, for example— probably because New Zealand is a well-stocked breeding ground. Australian horseracing has traditionally run off New Zealand breeding—horses such as Octagonal, Let's

Elope, and Doriemus are examples.

Now, however, we see more shuttle stallions from Europe, so New Zealand has far less influence over Australian racing than it used to. Bringing horses from Europe is no longer a big deal, and owners today spend a fortune on breeding horses in the purple (high quality blood line of both sire and mare), but it does not always pay off: some owners have picked up a horse for $8000 and netted $2 million from it. You just never know in racing—there are lucky horses, and there are excellent breeders (mares who have promised little on the racetrack) who just seem to click with the genes of a certain sire and produce a champion. The whole industry is based on the unpredictable. In general, though, bloodlines are important. The New Zealand bloodline, known as the Eight Carat bloodline, the one which produced Octagonal, has traditionally been very strong and a virtual guarantee of a good horse. Eight Carat was the mare, and she has produced brilliant progeny, as have her sisters.

In most cases, breeders look to the grandmother and mother to know what a mare will produce, but again, there is no sure-fire guarantee for producing a world-beater. There have been occasions where wealthy overseas owners have paid up to $7 million for a yearling that turns out unable even to trot. The bloodlines may look good, but some horses lack ability and motivation.

Generally, owners buy yearlings on the basis of the mare's performance; a good mare, it is thought, will produce good progeny. You can always get a pretty fair indication of a horse's merit from the mare; the sire is less important because their dominance in breeding is not as great, though the sire obviously does have an influence. If you get successful horses to breed, then percentages generally go the way of the breeder.

Breeders have a vested interest in the foals produced by bringing a champion sire to town and breeding it with their mares. So sire-fees can range from $500 to $300,000, depending upon the quality of the sire, what his progeny have recently done in terms of major race wins, and his strike rate. A good strike rate for a sire is considered very important for breeding, and a good sire can service up to 100 mares in a breeding season.

The foals are taken to the yearling sales and sold. The owners who purchase the horses generally have a trainer in mind, or they get the trainer to attend with them. The trainers can often tell the owners about good points and bad points, based on how the horse walks or how it is built. Generally, the owners will then fix a price—what their budget is, what they can afford, and what they think the horse will sell for.

After a successful sale, the yearlings are broken in, then sent to the stables to become familiar with stable conditions. Afterwards, the horses have a 6-week spell, and then their education begins. Most horses are 14 to 15 months old when they go to the yearling sales (a horse's official birthday is always designated as 1 August) and they will start barrier trials (two-year-old barrier trials) in September.

Horses that are born near August are obviously much closer to being actual two-year-olds when they start barrier trials than others are; some may be born as late as December, and they tend to be late developers for that reason. That extra two or three months can make all the difference.

The horses go through a kindergarten period—learning to gallop, familiarising themselves and becoming comfortable with the barriers. Generally the work is not hard because the horses' bones are still tender; if horses are stressed too early, they can get shin soreness because their bones are soft, and then they have to be put out for a spell.

The Golden Slipper, run in March, is Sydney and Australia's major two-year-old event (a group 1 race). The Melbourne equivalent is the Blue Diamond. Lead-up races for the Slipper begin in September and October, and some of these are qualifying races. The Slipper is based on invitation—because of either prize money or qualification. Prize money is generally the key, but a horse would need to have won $80,000 to $90,000 to be invited to be one of the 16 runners in the race.

Because of the significance of those first two years in a racehorse's life, breeding has become a specialist field within racing, and it contributes greatly to the overall success of the industry. Without good horses, the industry could not hold public interest in competition, especially when there are so many alternative gambling opportunities.

* * * * *

Of course, without trained horses, the racing industry would be nothing. These noble task-bred beasts are raised and trained for one activity—to run between barrier and winning post at blitzkrieg speed. Racehorses are nothing like the little ponies I grew up with: racehorses are by nature highly-strung and only happy at the gallop. They seem to know somewhere deep inside what they are bred for.

Trainers get horses at a young age—sometimes as yearlings or two-year-olds—and then must educate them, putting them in the barriers and showing them where to run. And racehorses are creatures of habit: if you teach and practise a skill over a long period of time, it becomes a deep-seated habit, and they begin to expect it to happen all the time. Of course, some horses get it into their minds that that is all they have to do. So trainers try to add some variety to the horses' work by running them in different ways. But certain elements of the horses' preparation never change: they must know how to be comfortable in the barriers, how to jump out hard when the gates open, and how to work at varying paces.

Horses cannot gallop full pace for a whole race, so in training we canter, then do some pace work and afterwards some sprinting. The animals are only so fit, and they cannot run all day. Consequently, trainers must prepare them carefully, judging the right mix of speed and distance in relation to fitness.

Horses have to be taught the various paces that the trainer wants them to travel at in a race. They are finely tuned animals, so their preparation is no different from that of a human athlete. They need to be physically and mentally ready before competing in an event. Because of the importance of a horse's preparation and condition, one of the crucial skills in race riding is to judge pace—to know with pin-point accuracy how long a horse should run at half, three-quarter, or full speed.

Jockeys master this skill by becoming familiar with the 200-metre marker poles on racetracks. Each 200-metre pole represents a furlong, so a 1200-metre gallop runs over six furlongs (six marker poles). The skill is to know how long a horse should take to run each furlong. A trainer might ask a jockey to go out onto the track and run 1200 metres with the first 600 at half pace. Half pace is usually 18 seconds to the furlong. The next 400 metres might be run at three-quarter pace (15 seconds to the furlong), and the last 200 metres at a working gallop (12 to 13 seconds to the furlong, although many horses can do it in 11 seconds.) Horses that race like the wind may get a gallop down to 10.5 seconds per 200 metres, but they are rare. When they come along, they are always worth a punt.

In the first months of your apprenticeship, you learn an exacting skill—to count one banana, two banana, three banana, and so on between 200-metre markers (per furlong). At full pelt, the horse has to run each furlong in twelve bananas. In the early days, jockeys find this a testing task. Often I only got to 15 bananas on a half-pace furlong and had to quickly blur through 16, 17 and 18 bananas (who said racing is not an exacting science?). After a year or so, though, a jockey leaves the bananas back in his race bag and unconsciously knows what the times and distances are. Even today, I can keep track of every second in a minute without a watch.

Racehorses are worked to the clock. Trainers know that a horse can only run so many seconds over a certain distance. For instance, 39 seconds for 600 metres is an average training gallop. Jockeys must work with trainers to judge this pace, because the horses' fitness levels are all-important. If you overwork a horse, you can irreparably harm the animal. They are a beautiful part of God's creation. And without these finely tuned racing instruments, the whole industry would falter—punters, jockeys and trainers. There is no future in over-stressing a racehorse.

Horses are clever animals, too; much more subtle than we might think. Horses know how to do the bare minimum of work to get the job done. Many pull up around the winning post or simply run the distances they have been set in training. They genuinely are creatures of habit. Others love to run in one part of the track—that love may prove detrimental to the animal's performance in a race, so indulging it would be a bad idea. (Punters rightly expect jockeys to call the shots, not horses.)

Consequently, jockeys must know what their animals are thinking all the time. This makes competitive racing far more complex than it looks—a jockey must be aware of the trainer's instructions, the other competitors, the unpredictable and often trying conditions of a race, and the subtle mind of the horse he or she rides. In that complex vortex of intersecting wills and decisions, a race is won or lost. Jockeys who do not remain four steps ahead of their mounts are unlikely to be successful; it is the jockey's job to get the horse to where he or she wants it to go before the horse even realises what is going on. So racing becomes a mind game involving judging what the horse is thinking, knowing how it will respond to commands, and getting it to appreciate the jockey's will.

But the best-laid plans often go awry, and horses cannot always be trusted to do what you tell them. I have had horses take off on me without my commanding them to do so, and plenty of horses have bucked me off. The number of times I have been thrown is too many to remember: if a horse wants to get you off its back, it will find a way to do so. Horses are capable of running their own race, and, especially as an apprentice, a jockey may lack the strength to hold them. Fighting to subdue this powerful beast, your arms pretty soon feel like jelly. A battle of wills between jockey and horse is not won by brute strength; if you try that caper, the horse will win every time. Contests of will are won in the mind. Good jockeys learn to out-think the horse.

* * * * *

The punter is another crucial part of the racing equation. Some punters are professionals; they gamble as a business. They study the form, pore over the video footage, and follow the guides and computer analysis religiously.

Then there is the mug punter, who simply picks up the paper or a form guide and says, 'Oh, there's a good jockey. I'll back him!' The percentages are heavily stacked against the mug punter; going merely by numbers or colours is a sure-fire way to lose your money in racing. Some punters even go by star signs. Recently, at a race in Brisbane, I had a lady approach me to tell me that there were no good Scorpios around in racing at the moment. 'So I can't bet,' she said.

Punters can be very superstitious, as I found out in Hong Kong and at Randwick at a recent mid-week meeting. On that day—it was towards the end of my career—a punter approached me. There were so few people there that you could have shot a cannon and hurt no one. This man stood on the fence and looked at me. (I tried to avoid eye contact with the public throughout my career because it just eggs on the lunatics.) But this guy was there on the fence, and he looked as if he was down to his last dollar and had had a shocker of a day. I was riding the number one horse in the race, and because of my following, the odds were very short (about $2.20 for the win). The guy looked at me as I rode in after my win, then his eyes shifted back to the tote-board, and then back to me, and finally back to the tote-board. Finally, he caught my eye and said, 'And you say God is real!' At $2.20 for the win he could not believe that God existed; he had expected about $4.80!

If you fail to bring home the bacon, punters can be very grumpy and abusive. They curse you, call you names—I seemed doomed to be tagged as a 'Bible basher'. These guys have paid $5 to get in to the track, and they feel that that gives them the right to say whatever they want to say, and if you lose more of their money on the tote, then you are worthless in their eyes. If you catch their eye, you are sure to cop some, but most of those punters speak out of their pockets; they can hardly see past the nose on their face. If you used the whip with your right hand, and they couldn't see that, they will yell: 'Why didn't you use the whip, Beadman?' You can please some of the people some of the time…

Some punters have reason to yell at you. Sometimes you do have a bad trot, break it, and then come out on another favourite and get beaten again. Punters do not count on that, and they can get abusive. When they line the fence, you keep your head down, because once one starts, they all start. It can feel like being in the middle of a riot. I have seen blokes throw beer bottles, glasses, and many other things. But you can't respond with even a word or a gesture, because if you do, the stewards will discipline you for bringing racing into disrepute.

* * * * *

In general, racing is a cash business, so the potential for criminal activity is ever present. Money is undoubtedly still laundered at the track; certainly in the old days crooks used the track to wash black money. Consequently the authorities are always vigilant, and today if you make a wager over $10,000, it must be declared. Declaration means that the person who accepts the bet must know where it comes from and who is putting it on. All bets must be identified, so now there is a much better record of where the money comes from and where it goes to. The authorities seem to have most bases covered.

The most recent evidence of corruption in racing came in the infamous Jockey Tapes episode, where a man dressed in a slick up-town suit regularly bet $50,000 at a Wednesday race meeting. It didn't take long for people to smell a rat: who comes to the races dressed in a really nice suit and bets $50,000 every Wednesday? It was a little out of the ordinary, and unlikely to go undetected.

A few jockeys, including Jim Cassidy, Kevin Moses, and Gavin Eades, were given time because of the Jockey Tapes. I am not sure what the authorities assumed, but at the very least the guys were identified as tipping horses to a gentleman the police were investigating. Jockeys can tip, but not for financial gain, and the police had recorded over 4,000 hours of this man's phone conversations in relation to a drug deal. He had talked to a jockey on a mobile phone, and the investigation went from there.

These days, jockeys cannot take money from people

and get away with it. I personally have heard of stewards placing microphones on the inside of a racetrack to record what goes on out on the course. The chances of illegality are slim, but that is not to say that it never goes on. Wherever there is money, there is bound to be criminal intelligence and crooked ingenuity. Corruption can never be completely obliterated, but I feel the authorities do a very good job of preventing it.

I have had the odd guy on the street—always a total stranger—approach me about fixing races. This was some 12 years ago, when I was still an apprentice. Once the word gets out that you cannot be bought, the crims give you a wide berth. You lay those foundations for precisely this reason: to keep your nose clean later. If you will not be bought, you will never be approached, but if you associate with criminals, you undoubtedly will get yourself into trouble.

Hong Kong was a tragedy for me because I was accused of something that I had tried hard to keep away from. Theo Green taught me to be a good person and an honest jockey, and I had tried to live up to that legacy. To have people doubt me later was crippling. You wonder what people think of you at the best of times, but during that period it was much worse, and the newspaper reports about me were in some cases quite scurrilous.

At times like that you rely on your friends to get you through. People you know, trust, and love stand with you through thick and thin. I was fortunate in that I had many racing friends.

6

FACES

Thinking about Mother Teresa, as I often do, and realising that by all the odds she will one day be canonised, I try to sort out the various characteristics in her of a saint.

MALCOLM MUGGERIDGE, CONVERSION

FACES

Name any profession. Choose any sporting endeavour worth pursuing: the people who grease its cogs and wheels are the ones we admire and imitate. Without heroes, sport lacks excitement—and notoriety. No sport is of much interest without the legends it produces.

This is surely true of racing. Stories of real people generate the intrigue and mystery of the sport. What would rugby be without David Campese or League without Peter Sterling? What would the Melbourne Cup be without Bart Cummings? Without these unique personalities, all our sports would lose something of their mystique, flamboyance, glamour and, finally, their appeal.

I have been enormously fortunate (and I count it a great privilege) that my career in racing has given me access to some of the really genuine industry characters. And without exception, they have marked my life in profound and interesting ways.

The first racing-world face to stick in my mind is Ron Quinton's. While I was growing up, dreaming of becoming a champion jockey, Ron was my hero. I later modelled my career on his, because he was the leading jockey in Sydney for eight seasons. The Boss had trained him, and Ron seemed a similar sort of man to myself: he was diligent, loved the industry, and was committed to the discipline and rigour that success demands.

I was in the second year of my apprenticeship—around 17 years of age—when I started to reap a bit of success for myself in racing. At that stage, the Boss would often warn me that to be successful you needed an old head on young shoulders. But old heads on young bodies are few and far between.

For a young jockey, when success starts to flow, when income rolls into your AJC trust account, when people begin to take your riding seriously, when the media start to write you up and put raps on you in television and radio interviews; it all becomes a little overwhelming. I started to believe my own press clippings, and got a little too big for my boots. One day, Ron Quinton decided to put some much-needed perspective into my fledgling career.

Ron was the consummate professional, and a genuine hard man of the track (there is a soft side to Ron, but on race day he is a pretty tough cookie), so he knew very well how to throw his weight around and keep some of the younger guys guessing. He had an imposing presence, and on the track he knew exactly how to bluff people out of a run they might otherwise have taken.

Apprentice jockeys are generally in awe of the older, track-proven, seasoned riders, which gives the older guys an additional edge. It is an unspoken law, but adhered to nonetheless, that in a race, the older guys can chop you off a little and take a few advantages they might not permit each other.

Ron and I were riding in a race at Warwick Farm on this day, and I was still a new up-and-comer, a young Turk. Even though Ron was my hero, I was trying to flex my own racing biceps. I wanted to win. Ron chopped me off in a race (crossing my path through a half opening to get to the fence and give his horse a better run). True, there was an opening and the position was not fully mine, but as his manoeuvre hampered my progress, he was not entitled to take the crossing. I held him out for as long as I could, but he shaved me, so I relinquished the position and lost my ground.

The stewards have upwards of eight cameras following a race, so very little eludes their prying eyes. They have all the angles covered, and if there is any interference to stop a horse's progress, the stewards don't hesitate to call an inquiry. Having been summoned over the PA system, Ron and I marched into the stewards' room, where six or seven stern-faced men, led by the chairman, made polite inquiries about the race and our apparent altercation.

They began with me. With great machismo I decided that Ron was not going to get away with his aggressive riding or push me around on the racetrack. I told the stewards exactly what had happened. I had observed how the more experienced jockeys handled these issues—they always stood their ground. I did exactly that and, of course, dumped Ron right in it.

The stewards turned to Ron, who said little except, 'Well, I'd really like to look at the film before I make any comment.' Ron taught me some wisdom that day: there is no point sticking your neck out until you know what the stewards have on you. Ron refused to dig a grave for himself—I had already unpacked the shovel and the stewards were preparing to administer the last rites. He wanted to see what he could or could not say in his own defence.

We looked at the film, and though it was clear that he had shaved me, it was equally clear that the story had grown dramatically in my retelling. If looks could kill, I would have been dead at that moment.

The stewards now asked Ron what he had to say. In the best traditions of jockeys' truth, Ron tried to snow them with a cock-and-bull story that even his mother would not have swallowed. (Ron is a great talker—the Perry Mason of jockeys—and this, even by his high standards, was a virtuoso performance.) He almost convinced the stewards that black was white. Almost, but not quite.

The stewards shooed us out of the room while they considered their verdict. Ron was Sydney's pre-eminent jockey, the kingpin. He was in his late twenties, and I was 17. I was terrified of him. Outside, Ron leaned over me and thrust his eyeballs up against mine. He explained—in a few colourful sentences—that jockeys do not do what I had done. 'Don't you ever, ever do that to me again,' he said furiously. Then he hammered me with a barrage of choice words. The menace in his eyes made me wilt.

A few pathetic words fumbled from my mouth, 'Uh, I'm sorry, Mr Quinton.'

I rode for the rest of that day, but I felt dreadful. I went back to the Lodge at High Street, and tossed and turned all night. A mixture of fear, guilt and anxiety sloshed around in my stomach. I knew that I had done the wrong thing. I got up the next morning, rode track work, and worried about how I would face Ron on the track. What would I say to him? He was my hero and now I was unable to speak to him. So I decided to ring him up.

The phone rang twice. 'Hello, Mr Quinton, it's Darren Beadman. Can I come around and see you?'

His answer said it all. 'Yep. All right.' And he hung up.

I was terrified, but I grabbed a taxi to his house and rapped on his door. Ron answered the door and mumbled, 'Come in.' It was the spider talking to the fly.

We sat down in his back room; it was the first time I had been in his house. I felt even more intimidated being there—it was his turf, his home territory. His trophies and his racing photos surrounded me. I began to explain everything to him, and as I did, I broke down and cried. I told him that I was sorry for what I had done.

Ron recognised my sincerity, and from that day on he looked out for me, assisted me, and encouraged my career. Ron became one of my major supporters. He eventually took over from The Boss as the trainer at High Street, and he was the one who gave me rides when I first came back from my Hong Kong ban.

Even now, I go to Ron for advice. He is a great horseman and a magnificent trainer because he is the professional's professional. He takes deep pride in his work. But Ron is more than that to me. When I see Ron's face, I see a true friend—someone I can rely on and trust.

* * * * *

Bob Hawke, one of Australia's great Prime Ministers, is another face I remember from my time in racing. Bob was absolutely sold on the industry and loved a punt, and he certainly helped the whole racing fraternity—particularly breeders, who benefited from the new international opportunities he opened up.

Bob seemed an ordinary bloke to the average punter on the street, and he kept that common touch throughout his political career. People viewed him as the working man's PM, and in that guise he often appeared at the races and mingled comfortably with the owners and trainers. Sometimes he asked about this horse's chances or that horse's form, but mostly he didn't need to ask: the trainers and owners were happy to volunteer their opinions.

When you saw his form guide, you realised he was serious about punting—it was marked with ink from ripped corner to smudged margin, with a cross or a tick next to each horse's name. He had his own system of shorthand, but there ended up being more ink spilled on his page than form to follow. So serious was Bob that one day his secretary rang me to ask for a tip. I was stunned that the PM's secretary had time to ring me for a tip, so I gave him my best ride for the day. (Tipping is acceptable in racing as long as it is not done for financial gain.) That was Bob Hawke: he just loved racing.

* * * * *

I first met Bart Cummings through my apprenticeship at Clear Day Lodge on High Street. Bart trained his horses at Leilani Lodge, the stables next door to us, so we shared Randwick. I raced a few horses for Bart in my apprenticeship. He had his own stable jockeys, but I was often his second or third stringer and he rang me if he

With my sister Belinda at our home in Garran, Canberra.

A sunny afternoon in the garden at home.

Pony Club–to think that 'The Boss' saw anything wrong with my riding style.

Lyneham Primary School Rugby First XV, 1976. Me front row, first from left.

Inspired on the rails winning his first barrier trial at Canterbury, 1984.

The Green apprentice learns to be a world-class jockey at Royal Randwick.

The young apprentice comes to grips with his first champion horse - winner of the 1984 Golden Slipper, the mighty Inspired.

Our three beautiful children, Jessica, Mitchell and Rachel, 1997.

The family gathers trackside for one of my many farewells.

With Kim celebrating my Hong Kong Bowl win in 1997.

The winning team in the Hong Kong Bowl, 1996.

The runners in the International Bowl in 1996. Me, third from left back row.

With Bart winning the Hong Kong International Bowl in 1997 on Catalan Opening.

Bringing it home past the big screen. Catalan Opening wins!

This is Your Life 1997

I should have known that Mike Munro wouldn't be at Wyong without a good reason.

Giving the glory to God, 1997.

My farewell at the Moonee Valley Race Club, 1997

The giant farewell cards.

An emotional goodbye to the generous Victorian fans.

An overwhelming number of signatures.

My parting speech.

was short of a jockey for any reason, so our friendship and professional involvement have evolved since the early 1980s.

My first ride for Bart was in the Doncaster Handicap, in which I rode a filly called More Rain. But things really got going between us when I won the 1990 Melbourne Cup on Kingston Rule, one of Bart's horses.

Ten days before the Cup, I rode five winners and two seconds from seven races at Rosehill, so my name was on everyone's lips. Bart had his choice among three jockeys to ride Kingston Rule, but he finally settled on me, and I took the ride (of course!) and won.

On the Saturday before Melbourne Cup Tuesday, I rode Kingston Rule for Bart in the Dalgety Handicap. It would be our final hit out before the Cup, and I was singing with excitement—I had ridden in the Cup before, but never on a horse with a reasonable chance of winning.

For the Dalgety Handicap, Bart instructed me to ride Kingston Rule back in the middle of the field, to let him relax and enjoy the run, and to let him come home strong. He finished by adding, 'If you've got a chance to win, then win. But don't push him—remember, the main race is on Tuesday. If you're going to be beaten, don't knock him about.' I followed Bart's instructions to the letter, and brought him home down the outside. He came in second, but I didn't pull the whip on him.

Some people, particularly disgruntled punters and a few members of the press, criticised me for not whipping the horse; they felt that I had taken it too easy. The stewards had no problem with the ride, though, because they could see I was pushing him. But that is Australian racing—Aussies love to see a thrashing with the whip.

They need to know that you are doing everything humanly (and legally!) possible. A few argued that if I had hit him with the whip, we would have won. After all, he was the favourite.

When I came back in off the track, I told Bart, 'He'll be a good chance for the Cup, you know. He gave me such a good feeling—he was so strong. He's a good shot for this year's Cup and even next year's.' The horse had potential. I could see he was going to mature into a top horse.

'Don't worry about next year's Cup,' said Bart. 'Let's get this one over and done with!'

I prayed that Tuesday would be dry, because Kingston Rule was dead meat on a wet track. Tuesday rolled around and it was a perfect day. The horse drew barrier one, and the rest is history.

Bart and I celebrated all night long. Our friendship grew new legs that day, and has since blossomed further. Over the years, Bart has demonstrated loyalty, wisdom and confidence in my career. I trust his judgement implicitly; not only about horses—though he has one of the best horse-brains in the world—but about life, too.

But Bart is best known for his astute assessment of horses. On cool, crisp autumn mornings, should you have the privilege of watching him observe his horses, you can see their potential through his eyes. He works his horses with wisdom and sound judgement; he knows exactly when to push them and when to let them progress at their own pace.

Bart Cummings is the ultimate trainer. TJ 'Tommy' Smith won more trainers' premierships, but Tommy had the numbers on his side. The sheer number of horses he had, coupled with his undoubted expertise on the track, won him those premierships. But Bart is the man for the big race—he is the Cup's undisputed king. Having won the Melbourne Cup 10 times, Bart is a true legend of the industry.

* * * * *

Gai Waterhouse took over training horses from her father, Tommy Smith. Gai is well known for her flamboyant dress sense on the track and her astute mind when it comes to racing thoroughbreds. Gai and I have had a long connection. I have ridden many of her horses, and in 1996 she approached me to become the equivalent of a stable jockey, doing most of her riding for her. I declined the offer because I wanted to be free for any stable. (I had similar offers from John Hawkes and Bart Cummings, too, and turned them down for the same reason.) I felt my career was best handled if I remained freelance. I have had a good business association with Gai over the years, and have brought home many winners for her.

Gai is a diligent worker. She has children and a family to care for, but she still gives her heart and soul to training horses. Gai oozes energy. She stays focused on her work, and her determination is second to none.

There is no better example of Gai's grit than the history of the struggles she endured to get her training licence. When Robbie Waterhouse, Gai's husband, lost his licence, Gai was determined to pick up the slack by gaining hers. Throughout that ordeal, she always looked tired, but she kept pressing on, like a greyhound chasing a rabbit. She never gave in. Gai was a genuine inspiration to me because she kept on pursuing her dream—and she achieved it.

Gai knows her horses, too, so she was an excellent trainer to ride for. In fact, her horses are much like her—fit, determined, and bred to go through brick walls. Gai's horses never quit, and my guess is that she trains her horses to run their races in the same way that she lives her life—hard and fast.

Gai's husband Robbie was disqualified because he was judged to be associated with the Fine Cotton affair—that infamous Australian horse-switching scandal. He was found guilty and sentenced to a lifetime ban from racing. When Robbie tried to come back from the ban, Gai stood up and backed her convictions. She was there with him all the way, and I greatly admired her for her dogged courage against all odds.

I have met Robbie several times, and while I have not had a lot to do with him, I have always had a good feeling about the man. I know little of Robbie's life, but he has done nothing wrong by me. I believe in treating people as you would like to be treated, and in my book, the racing industry has dealt harshly with Robbie.

I hope that some day the authorities overturn his ban, because Robbie has done his time, no matter what actually happened. No one should be left dangling permanently from the hangman's noose. I feel that it is time to grant Robbie a reprieve, but I suppose some of racing's powers-that-be disagree. Undoubtedly, there would be some who want to see him reinstated and some who are adamantly opposed. The nays must still have the numbers.

* * * * *

Jack and Bob Ingham go back a long way with me, and I freely acknowledge that if they pulled out of racing, it would leave a major hole in the business. They do a lot for racing and a lot for the community. They are the big-time owners of racehorse flesh (and chicken flesh) in Australia. Without them, something would indeed be lacking from the Australian racing scene.

I first met them when I was apprenticed to The Boss. Jack came around on Friday afternoons to visit our stables in his role as an AJC committee member. The Boss trained the Inghams' horses, so visits were mandatory. After his committee meetings, we pulled his horses out of the High Street stables and walked them for him. Jack loves racing. He breathes it. He admires the horses, relishes a punt.

On the other hand, we hardly ever saw Bob. In fact, during the entire period of my apprenticeship, I probably met him twice. He seems to have become more prominent in the scene since the development of Crown Lodge and Woodlands; before that he may have preferred a backseat role.

The Inghams were heavily involved in trotting before they moved into the gallops. In moving to racehorses, they became the most important owners for me: I have raced more horses for them than for any other owners.

The Inghams have always supported me, always given me opportunities and chances. One major opportunity was the job of stable jockey at Crown Lodge in the late 1980s, where I worked for around two years. Though we had great success, I had an unfortunate falling out with the trainer, Vic Thompson, and because it is easier to get a new jockey than a trainer, we parted company.

Still, while the position lasted—and afterwards, as well—I had the chance to really get to know the Inghams, and I found both Jack and Bob to be outstanding men. They have had a huge influence on my life. Because of the unique relationship I had shared with Jack, he was one of the first people I rang to announce my retirement from racing.

* * * * *

Shane Dye is a man you either love or hate. He is different, but we get on like a house on fire. He first came to Australia from New Zealand in 1985, when I was still in France. Since then, he has established himself as one of Australasia's leading horsemen.

Of course, when I came back from France, we had some great stoushes on the racecourses of Australia. Our personal competition and rivalry on the course have been intense. Though I have had little to do with Shane socially, I have been to a few concerts with him and found I enjoyed his company.

We have very different lifestyles, so it was certainly not inevitable that we became friends. In fact, it was especially difficult, because for most of our overlapping careers we have been Australia's first and second jockeys. The media (and others) seemed to want to play us off against each other. It would have been easy to make Shane just a rival, but that approach would have proved detrimental to our relationship. Shane and I chose not to operate that way. We chose to treat each other as we both wanted to be treated—with respect.

As mentioned, we have had some great duels on the track. But despite these battles, the key to our relationship is that we speak well of each other—even as competitors. When I won the 1996 Melbourne Cup on Saintly, Shane rode Gai Waterhouse's horse Nothin' Leica Dane. At the post-race interview, I told the packed media conference that I followed the best jockey in the race, Shane Dye, shadowing his moves because I knew that if I followed him, I would be there or thereabouts at the finish. 'Shane's an excellent judge of pace,' I told them, 'so if he was up there at the front or way back in the pack, he'd be there for a reason.' Shane was in fact in a forward position—which suited me—and, as I said, I knew he would not be there without good reason, so I followed him. Shane is a smart jockey; he does little without carefully considering his options, and his anticipation is electric. Shane judges 50 metres down the track as if it were five metres. Shane was the jockey that helped me win the race, I told the media, because he took me into the action.

After the interview, Shane came up to me and thanked me for what I had said. I saw in his eyes that it meant something to him. But it was how I felt. There was no point claiming all the glory, because Shane truly is a magnificent horseman, a real champion.

That episode taught me the importance of speaking well of others. And lest anyone think this is a one-way street, it is not. Shane has always spoken well of me. He did so recently when he raced a little three-year-old called Tie The Knot. I had won some serious races on him, but it was Shane who raced him to victory in the Sydney Cup. He knew that I had done all the patient preparation with the horse, so he thanked me publicly for that.

A lot of people, however, think of Shane as outspoken and brash. Don't get me wrong—Shane is opinionated. But he is also very good at what he does, and he can afford to be vocal. Nevertheless, the average Aussie seems to prefer the underdog, the battler, the guy who is humble (or at least seems to be), to the tall poppy who speaks his mind. Shane is not cast from that mould and never will be, and I suspect this fact alone explains some of the public and media antipathy. Shane pursues his point of view aggressively, but when you get to know him, you find that deep down he is a tremendous bloke. His brashness is part of him, part of what makes him Shane Dye. He means nothing by it—it is just his style, and it has its positives and negatives. One fact remains certain, though: on the track, Shane is certain of everything he does.

* * * * *

Lester Piggott is an icon of racing. Before I met him, I had heard about him, read about him, and seen him on television. Lester was many people's hero, the epitome of the punter's jockey. I met him at Rosehill and had my picture taken with him. I felt like a groupie, and felt embarrassed about that later, but Lester remembered me from France, so we got together and had a bit of a chat.

At that meeting, I reminded Lester of a very funny incident at Evry in France in a distance race. Lester was one of my heroes, so I was following him. He was three off the lead on the fence, but at the halfway mark, he was stuck in a pocket and couldn't get out. What he did floored me.

I was trying to follow him, and to watch what he was doing—to learn from a master. I noticed he had an extra long whip—it was the length of a two-wood. (Europe permits the use of longer whips than ours.) Lester hit the horse on his outside, because it was blocking him, up the tail. The horse kept on blocking him, and finally Lester gave it a good slap. Whoosh—the horse bolted. It took off and its jockey had absolutely no idea what hit him. Lester then slipped out of the pocket, and his horse went on to win!

Unfortunately for me, I only took half of Lester's trick on board, and it nearly cost me. When I was in a similar position in a race, I tried a few short, sharp jabs up a horse's rear end. I kept flicking up its tail—that worked, but I failed to win the race. When I came back to the jockey's room, the PA announcer summoned me to the stewards.

The stewards asked me about an occurrence at the 1200-metre mark, but I didn't know what was wrong; I simply had no idea that what I had done was illegal. So they showed me the film, and I saw it as plain as the nose on my face. There I was, in full glory, flicking a horse up the tail. To say the least, the stewards were extremely interested in my activities. Jockeys never lie, of course, so, with a poker face, I told them that my whip had become caught in the horse's tail and I was jerking it free.

The stewards fell for it and let me go. What I desperately needed to learn then was how Lester got away with it. What I had neglected to copy was Lester's whip— it was brown, and on film, it blended in with the horse. My Australian whip was white, and waving a white whip is like waving a white flag emblazoned with the words 'look at me'. From that day on, I used a brown or black whip.

* * * * *

I have had an association with Alan Jones for many long years. The Boss taught us to accommodate the media, and with Alan doing just that was truly a pleasure. I had little to do with Alan until I won the Melbourne Cup in 1990. He reached me through my family, asking if he could do an interview. I rang back and said fine, and we did the interview. Who knows if Jonesy backed my horse, but he seemed pretty happy about the ride.

From that day on we have been friends. Though we do not see each other a lot, it has been a firm relationship. We have had some outstanding dinners together and I have always enjoyed his warm company, good humour, and genuine sense of integrity.

Alan has committed himself to helping young people in many fields of endeavour. You only have to listen to his show to be impressed by the support he gives young Australians. When I had the problem in Hong Kong and returned with such a dark cloud over my head, he called up and invited me to dinner. Jonesy did only one thing that whole night: he gave me encouragement about what had happened, and about my future. He showed me that he still believed in me and that he cared. He also defended me publicly on the airwaves. His efforts made my reintroduction into Australian racing much easier. I admire Jonesy for that because he had no personal motive to do so. He was a friend when I really needed one.

* * * * *

The man they call 'Shadow' is none other than Graham McNeice. Graham was the first person to interview me, so he has some unique footage. He filmed me as a 15-year-old because The Boss told him, 'You'd better get some footage of this young man.' Graham was working at Channel 10 at the time. After that, I always accommodated him; my first interview in a television studio was for Graham at Channel 10. Since then, he's been a loyal friend to me on and off the track, and a major influence on my career thanks to his encouragement and support.

* * * * *

And what would racing be without horses? What would my career have been without my four-footed friends? My first really important horse was Inspired, on whom I won the 1984 Golden Slipper. Inspired put my name on the map, but people came to know me more because of his ability as a horse than mine as a jockey. The Boss trained him, and I educated him and prepared him for racing.

Inspired was a spirited animal; highly-strung, and extremely strong for his age. Even as a two-year-old, he raced more like a late three-year-old; he was a well-developed horse, and it showed in his racing—he was too good for his competitors.

Kingston Rule made my career in 1990. From 1984 to 1990 I was among the top five horsemen in Australia, but I never quite reached the heights I had dreamed of. So I was rarely offered champion horses to ride. But Kingston Rule changed all that; my career made a complete 180-degree turn, and my stocks steadily rose from 1990 on—until Hong Kong.

Super Impose was a Melbourne horse trained by Lee Freedman, but he had most of his success in Sydney. He won the Epsom and the Doncaster, so he had quite a reputation before I took him on. His owner wanted someone to ride him all the way through. He was a very different horse from Inspired—laid-back and relaxed. He was so relaxed that I sang songs to him before he went into the barriers (Darryl Braithwaite's 'Horses' was one of his particular favourites.) He was a lovely horse, but he had a very unusual racing pattern. He sat back in his races at first, and then, when he was ready, stormed down the outside and blew the opposition away.

It was this distinctive style of his that produced what I consider to be my greatest ride—the 1991 Epsom Handicap. He was running last (out of 20-odd horses) with 600 metres to go. His normal pattern was to barnstorm on the outside, but I elected to take him back inside. I came from the back of the field to the front along the inside of the runners and made the decision to weave through the horses from last on the home corner to hit the lead at the 20-metre mark—he won the race by a length and a half. There were 20 000 people there, and we received a standing ovation coming back in. He had won the Epsom-Doncaster previously, so he was shooting for the double again. No horse had ever done that before on four major miles, but he did it.

Octagonal is one of the greatest horses Australian racing has ever seen. But he was a trial; not an easy ride. He only ever gave you as much as you wanted. Though he always had plenty of petrol in the tank, he never stretched himself if there was a simpler way home. His biggest winning margin was probably a length and a quarter—he always seemed to pip someone else by a short half head or a nose.

He was a pulse-pounder to ride, because if you left your run too late, he would never get you there. On the other hand, if you took off too early, he would stop halfway and not continue on. He seemed to wait—he had obviously long since realised that he only had to win by a nose. So with him there was always only a fine line between success and failure, but you couldn't question his smarts. He had brains. He also had character, his own unique personality.

Octagonal is at stud now, and he has a huge strike rate of successful siring. He is a shuttle stallion, serving six months in Australia and six months in France. In fact, he is really the first Australian horse to have this honour.

In my view, Octagonal has done wonders for racing. He won the Triple Crown and the four major group 1 races. People love a champion, and he is an undisputed champion. He brought people back to the sport—particularly young people. (For some reason, young people in the 1980s seemed to lose interest in racing.) Having a connection with Octagonal did wonders for my career, too; people noticed me because I rode him.

Toward the end of his career, the champion tag was starting to fall off him. He lost a few races, and his stud price was tumbling. I had elected not to race him in Melbourne, because I had my own career to pursue in Sydney, but Jack Ingham sent me an SOS to jump a plane and race him. So I flew down and rode him at Caulfield in the Underwood Stakes, and we won. It was the greatest comeback since Lazarus. Octagonal was back, and finished his racing career a champion.

* * * * *

Without characters (two-legged and four), the racing industry could not draw the crowds who flock through the turnstiles of our metropolitan racetracks. If people only wanted to punt, they can do so in a pub or a club. It is personalities that bring people to the track. And without these, I doubt racing would have tugged at my heartstrings in the way that it did. I fell in love with this great sport and its heroes.

7

WINNING

Success is a journey, not a destination

BEN SWEETLAND

WINNING

If you are fortunate enough, as I was, to work with powerful horses such as Saintly, Super Impose, Octagonal and Kingston Rule, and fine trainers such as Bart Cummings, and supportive owners such as the Inghams, success will come your way as inevitably as day follows night. Your own talent is simply the icing on an already promising looking cake; winning takes care of itself.

Many magnificent characters supported me in my racing career—the owners who loved the sport enough to invest in it, the trainers who prepared the animals, the horses that carried me past those glorious winning posts, and the media who shared the news with hundreds of thousands of sympathetic punters. All these helped me towards the great milestones and wins of my career. I had set goals for myself when I was only a young boy, racing my pony at Lackey Park in Moss Vale, but to have achieved them is testimony, in my view, to the miracles granted by a loving God.

Winning is never an accident. Someone once said

that winning is everything. Another astute observer qualified the remark: winning is not everything—it is the only thing. I disagree. Winning is never the most important thing in life. I had to learn this lesson the hard way, of course. I won two Melbourne Cups, but those two wins could not have been more different, because I was different. How you win matters, but not as much as acknowledging why you win.

When I won my first Melbourne Cup on the Bart Cummings-trained horse Kingston Rule, I felt that I had done so by myself: relying on my own courage and ability, depending only on the horse's strength, and Bart's know-how.

And by the time I won that race, it was my time to win. Any earlier in my career and I doubt I could have ridden that race or have handled the responsibilities that came with such stunning success. I would have lacked the necessary wisdom or maturity to succeed with the ride in the midst of such fierce competition. Having raced several earlier Cups, I was finally ready to handle the pressure of the event and cope with the media's microscope.

It had been my dream, from the time I was a kid of ten, to win a Melbourne Cup. On Kingston Rule the dream came true. I felt that I had done it all on my own, because that's how I understood success at that time. When I hit the winning post in front of that enormous Flemington crowd, it was almost frustrating; there was no one there I could hug or grab or shout to. I was on my own with my sense of achievement. I realised quickly that achieving a dream is nothing without others to share the joy with.

Now, when I look back on this event, I can see that it, like everything else in my life, was no accident. I am where

I am today because there is a far greater purpose and mission planned for my life than I could have imagined then.

* * * * *

I was stable rider for Jack and Bob Ingham at the time of the 1990 Melbourne Cup. Jim Cassidy had been due to ride Kingston Rule in the Cup. He was one of three jockeys—myself included—that Bart Cummings was looking at. Then Jim was offered a ride on a different galloper, and he chose that instead. I had five wins from seven races leading in, so Bart picked me. (Jim probably felt sick in the stomach when Kingston Rule came home!)

My Cup Tuesday was a good one by industry standards: I had some good rides under my belt—three second-place finishes—leading into the main race. But I loathe running second. When you run second, you always ask yourself: What more could I have done? Who wants to go through that sort of torture? I would have preferred to run fourth or fifth—because then the soul-searching becomes futile. There is such a fine line between first and second, that you over-analyse the details of the race, whereas if you run fifth, you feel that no matter what you did, you still wouldn't have won.

Going into the Cup, my confidence was a little shaky because of those second-place finishes. I was putting added pressure on myself—I was sure the whole day was going against me. It also fired me up, though, because I did not want to make any mistakes in the big race. I demanded 100 per cent focus from myself. When I later watched footage of myself walking around the enclosure before the race, I could not believe what I was seeing; my face was so stiff and stern. I appeared almost angry, but it was just the intense focus—running the race the only thing on my mind.

In fact, I had been running the Cup race in my mind for weeks before the event, studying every detail, colour, sight, sound, and scent. I analysed the other jockeys, I thought about their strengths and weaknesses, I memorised their colours and the form of their animals. This is the information that gives you the edge on the day. I considered every possible contingency, the opposition, my horse, and the trainer's instructions.

The intensity of the Cup is unbelievable. In the race, you have to know exactly what is going on around you all the time. The preparation you do before the race is very deliberate and carefully programmed precisely because you have to make split-second decisions, with microchip accuracy on the day. Hours of study go into every race. This is a continuing investment that all jockeys make in their craft. The Melbourne Cup heightens the commitment.

Before the race, we jockeys put on new silk shirts in the colours supplied by the owners. In the jockeys' room, the atmosphere was electric—a thousand thoughts, glazed eyes and thumping hearts. I have ridden in many races, but the Melbourne Cup is definitely the big one. Noise, laughter and conversation normally liven up the jockeys' room, but on Cup day there's a stillness. Just tight lips and silent thoughts. Joviality is absent or suppressed.

Everyone puts media commitments on hold as race time approaches. The only talk comes from the stewards, who stop by to pronounce the same rules they give on every racetrack, on every race day, in every corner of the racing world. The penalties have been recited before, but each jockey listens very attentively this time, as if it was a major news break. The looks on our faces tell the story: studied, pensive. For each and every one of us, this moment is what all the training has been leading up to.

Then the jockeys leave the room and engage in small talk for five or ten minutes with the trainer and the horse's owners, and we all try to act as though our hearts aren't thumping fit to burst. At this point, the trainer will clarify instructions and listen to the jockey's race plan. Then they give you a leg up on the horse and you walk around the enclosure calming your nerves and settling your horse.

Horses feel the tension of their riders. They know when a jockey is stressed or nervous. The communication line between rider and horse is the reins. Tension in your hands, or uncertain vibes, channel straight through the bit to the horse's teeth and on to its spirit, like an electric current. The reins are a phone line, and unrelaxed hands transmit a 911 call straight to the animal's heart. Jockeys relax to keep their animals calm.

An affectionate pat on the head soothes the eager beast. The soft tone of the voice communicates the intensity of little more than training. The horse's confidence begins to rise and its emotions settle. Then the strapper will lead the horse out of the enclosure with the jockey on board. The crowd cheers; the PA is blaring. This may unsettle horse, rider, or both. But the trainer has put together a jockey and a horse with similar characters—a team that, with united hearts, will carry the owner's colours to victory.

* * * * *

When the moment finally arrived to start the race, I ran through a quick checklist of my Cup preparation program. The hard yards of readying myself were complete; it was time for review. In the Flemington enclosure I thought through the race, going over every detail again and again, until the officials came to lead Kingston Rule to the barriers.

Leaving the Flemington members' enclosure, we passed the public. They cheered and carried on like crazy, clearly enjoying the atmosphere and fun of this special November day. We gathered behind the barriers—at Flemington, they are near the car park. Some people tried to impress by yelling out comments inspired by high spirits and champagne seemingly. Some encouraged. Others bagged the jockeys and the horses.

We did our preliminary exercises, stretching and warming up. It was quiet behind the barriers. I think I wished one or two people a safe ride, but few words were exchanged. Before a race, there is normally a joke or two in the barriers, but not on Cup Tuesday. My eyes, if they caught anyone else's, met poker faces.

Once we hit the barriers, Kingston Rule knew that it would not be long before he flew out over 3200 metres, maybe to glory. He knew that he had been bred and trained for this. He walked straight in. To ease the load on his back and give him a breather, I propped up on the sides of the barrier, and we waited several minutes for the other horses to settle.

We had drawn barrier one. It was like a death sentence to draw that barrier. No horse had ever won the

Cup from there, so the statistics were against us. But races are never won by statistics; they are won by willing flesh, committed hands and hooves, and hearts full of desire and determination. And we were determined.

It was a warm day in Melbourne that November, and the horse's weight meant that I had had to waste hard, which was good. That preparation stirred my blood. It helped me. I wanted to taste the sweet wine of victory, which I had worked so hard for.

In those few moments before the gates fly open, a good racehorse begins to gather itself. Kingston Rule was no exception; I felt his legs pumping up and down like eager pistons. Like a good sprinter, he was gathering himself. Born with the lust to run, he was anxious to get going. It was everything I could do to keep him composed a little longer.

The starter got up on his stand, and when the gates clanged open, my heart pounded. The horses leapt out as if chased by the devil. The wind immediately bit our faces. We settled in around mid-field and paced ourselves for the metres ahead.

The first corner arrived in a rush. Jockeys were parrying for positions in the first 300 metres. After that, the dust settled and we held our ground, waiting for whatever surprises lay ahead. Having barrier one, I was happy to stay where I was. I could have gone to the lead, but I let others cross in front of me. I talked to Kingston Rule throughout race: 'Whoa, boy' was a constant refrain. I held him back and slowed his strong desire to dash to the front.

The sounds of a race ring truer for spectators than they do for jockeys. Spectators' hearts start racing at the sound of thundering hooves, but jockeys never hear that. A jockey's concentration carries him to another plane, and the only sounds to break the stillness are those of other jockeys, communicating with each other and cajoling their horses. 'I'm still here…' or 'I need a bit more room…' can be heard constantly. You hear horses and jockeys hitting the fence, the irons scraping the rails like fingernails screeching on a blackboard, but you never hear the hooves.

My heartbeat was steady throughout the race, but my adrenalin resisted any possibility of fatigue. For a few fleeting moments, you just are—your concentration takes over and you connect with something other. Your only thoughts are about the movements on the chessboard that is the race; racing is chess with a physical side. You try to ride not only your horse, but everyone else's, too.

Throughout the race, I kept Kingston Rule on the rails, and made him feel confident. A horse's confidence is vital in a race. If he is happy in his position, he will always perform well. Humans are the same—when we are confident, we perform. Midway through the race, I was still in the pack and was placed around sixth on the fence, six lengths off the lead. I remained there until the 600-metre mark. The horse didn't fight me; he just cruised along.

I didn't pass another horse until 200 metres from the finish. At the home corner, runners began to move out to make their run. I kept getting closer to the front—as blokes peeled off one by one, I took their positions. Finally I saw daylight ahead, up to the winning post. I kept moving up and saving ground. By the time I hit 200 metres from the finish, I knew that most guys had made their runs too early; their horses were flat, and had nothing left to give. I was able to move off the fence and get a run between them.

The Flemington straight is one of the longest in Australia. When you hit the front, and you know there is very little petrol left in the tank—your horse is running on momentum and heart, as Kingston Rule was—you realise how far away the winning post still is. It feels as if you are crossing the Nullarbor Plains, and the end is an eternity away. You simply wait for a horse to come at you. I knew that I was flat stick—Kingston Rule had nothing left to give.

But I didn't pull the whip on him. There was no need. I would have gained nothing—he was giving me all he had. It is immoral to ask for more than that. He kept going, and the Bart Cummings' polish got him home. Bart had made him run the miles in training and in races. He knew what it took for a horse to win at Flemington. Another horse came at me on the inside—The Phantom. I thought he had us: he made a rush, but he faded quickly. Suddenly the post loomed up, and we crossed it. We had won.

Hitting the winning post was such a rush, such a relief. We had done it! I threw my hand in the air (the stewards fined me $200 for dangerous riding because of that) to celebrate the win. I should have waited, but I couldn't. As we pulled up, jockeys called to me 'On ya', Dazz.' It was like a dream.

I trotted back to the scale. An official led me on toward the winner's circle. When Kingston Rule trotted into the enclosure, I was deafened by the cheering, clapping, catcalls and yells. The air was thick with roses that people were tossing from the stands. The 200-metre trot back past the rose garden, in front of a vast sea of racing fans in tails and silk dresses, left me breathless. I was so close to the public, and such a public outpouring of emotion is overwhelming.

Words cannot describe what I felt. If you ever have a dream that takes 14 years to fulfil, you will know what that Cup Tuesday was like for me. And I was just 24 years old.

The prize money for the win was $1.3 million—of which I received 10 per cent. The owner, David Hains, was thrilled, because the horse was home-bred, by an American sire out of an Australian mare that Hains owned. The horse was bred in the purple and had the pedigree of a champion; that day he proved it. Kingston Rule represented a big investment for Hains, probably hundreds of thousands of dollars. It was a big payday and richly deserved.

The Melbourne Cup is one of the biggest two-mile races in the world. It is global, and winning it thrusts you into the limelight right around the world. A few years ago, the race was won by a lot of old handicappers—good horses but a little out of form. Running on a low weight, they could win. But not any longer; today, you need a world-class galloper to win the race.

The media scrum after the race was unbelievable. All the television stations interviewed me. People never stopped congratulating me all day—it was continuous. I rode no other horses after the Cup, so I had a chance to really soak it all up, whereas if I had ridden again, I would have had to focus on that ride. Now I could just enjoy the fruits of winning.

That night, after the win, we celebrated as if there was no tomorrow. There was a special dinner—a party, really—and the press followed us there. I had to keep my weight down, as usual, so I only had a sip of a glass of champagne—I had races the next day, anyway. (I could have pulled the pin on that, but I decided not to, so I had to trek from Melbourne to Sydney the next day for the races at Canterbury.)

The party carried on from three in the afternoon until midnight or later. There was a continuous hullabaloo of raucous affirmation and praise and merry laughter. I felt as if I was on my wedding night again. But I was not; it was just one fleeting victory in life's long journey.

People wanted photographs, autographs, and anything else I would give them—mostly, my time. I had to get up early the next morning to meet my commitments at Canterbury. I won a double that day! I was on a complete adrenalin-rush the whole time, high on the ecstasy of winning one of the racing industry's golden prizes.

* * * * *

Flemington came just at the right time in my career. I was ready to act as a good steward of the resources that success would bring. True, I failed in Hong Kong, but my fall may have been greater had it not been for the years of preparation beforehand. Each and every platform prepares you to launch yourself out at a higher level. You are ready to handle new pressures—not only those that occur before a race, but also those that come after.

And the pressures of winning are enormous. People everywhere want a piece of you. You can't offend the media, of course, so you lose a little control over yourself and your own time. Declining an interview has to be done in just the right manner. You have to maintain a patient spirit, because if you fail to give the media time now, they won't bother coming back to you later. Tommy Smith had a very utilitarian attitude toward the media: he believed that media interviews were like hundreds of thousands of dollars of free advertising.

The win at Flemington led directly to my invitation to Hong Kong. It won me international acclaim, and in Australia it put me in the major league of jockeys. Hardly a soul in Australia misses the Melbourne Cup; winning makes you a household name.

But I still remembered where I came from. I never allowed my head to grow too big—I was still the Darren Beadman who had grown up in Canberra and Moss Vale. In fact, I don't think I ever fully appreciated the magnitude of what happened that day at Flemington, of what it meant to my career. I was certain of one fact, though; I had accomplished this Herculean feat through my own strength.

* * * * *

Winning my second Melbourne Cup in 1996 was another golden moment. There was less pounding in the heart because I had fulfilled my lifetime ambition in 1990. (Climbers say that Everest is never the same the second time.) The 1996 Melbourne Cup felt different for another major reason: I did not do it on my own. It was a dream to win two, but when the second one came, I knew where my blessings came from and why I had been given my gifts.

My life, my skills, even my ambitions, came from

elsewhere. When I rode back past the roses in 1996, the moment was magical, but by then I had a much deeper sense of life's great mysteries. My acceptance speech focused on one thing: giving God the glory for all that had happened in my life. I wanted to dwell on God and the Lord Jesus Christ because I am what I am by the grace of God.

Once you hand the reins of your life over to God, you see things in their true perspective. Success can change you, but once you know where success comes from, it is easier to cope with. You send the honours, the glories, the praises that go with success in a different direction. You never hold on to them; you hand them back to God. Then you start fresh and build again.

Success is wonderful, but not if you start to believe your own press and forget who you are and where you came from. Success can destroy you. I was heading down this dark, dangerous, slippery path until reality brought me crashing down in Hong Kong. Before I acknowledged God, success did change me to a certain degree. I truly believed that I had done everything through my own strength. But as the pastor said that day, 'You can't do it on your own.' And my life has not been the same since.

This new perspective shone all the way through to the punters in 1994–5 when I won the jockeys' premiership. I rode at Rosehill on the Saturday that I was to receive the trophy. That was the year I beat Bill Cook's record for most winners in the city. God had been doing things in my heart and stomach all day, so I knew that something was going to happen. I could sense it.

I sat in the jockeys' room at Rosehill, next to another jockey, Bruce Compton. Before all my rides, from 1994 onwards, I read my Bible and prayed in the jockeys' room. The Holy Spirit came over me as I sat in the room that day. My eyes started to well up with tears. I was fearful that Bruce would ask me a question, and that God would expose what was going on in my heart. Bruce called my name and I looked up. He saw the moisture in my eyes and said no more.

God spoke to me then. It is difficult to describe; I simply knew deep inside what God wanted. 'I want you to read a Scripture today, and that will describe your life. I want you to read Psalm 116.' My spirit knew what God was asking. Reading Psalm 116 was not exactly what I had in mind for my speech, so I asked God, 'Why do you want me to read that?'

God answered me clearly: 'Because this Psalm will explain your life to the people—where you come from, where you are going, and what I have done in your life. People are wondering why you are a Christian.' I had never read that Psalm before, so I opened up to Psalm 116—and panicked. It is 19 verses long! I looked at the next Psalm. Psalm 117 has only two verses and less than 20 words. 'Why, Lord, can't it be 117 instead?'

> *I love the Lord for he heard my voice;*
> *He heard my cry for mercy.*
> *Because he listened to me,*
> *I will call on his name as long as I live.*
> *Death looked me in the eye;*
> *Hell was hard on my heels.*
> *I was overcome by trouble and sorrow;*
> *Then I called on the name of the Lord:*
> *'Oh Lord, save me!'*

God takes the side of the helpless;
When I was at the end of my rope, he saved me.

O Lord, truly I am your servant;
I am your servant...
You have freed me from my chains
I will lift high the cup of salvation – a toast to God!
I'll complete what I promised God I'd do,
And I'll do it together with his people.

I left the jockeys' room to walk down and receive my award for winning the premiership. I stepped out into the enclosure with my Bible. People gave me strange looks; they must have been wondering what on earth I had in my hands.

After the winning trainer received his award, it was my turn. I first thanked the Lord, then everyone else who had assisted me. Then I told the crowd that I wanted to share with them what God had done in my life, and that God had asked me to do it to explain my life.

The Psalm speaks about being in a place of death and moving to a place of life. That had happened to me in Hong Kong and after. I had had no life.

When I started reading it out to the crowd, the words hit me afresh. I could not have described my life to people in any better way; that Psalm said it all. Seven or eight thousand people were present at Rosehill, and you could have heard a pin drop. Even guys at the betting ring stopped and watched the event on the television.

I did it because God wanted me to. People rang me for days afterwards about the Psalm. I was a little embarrassed about doing it, but once I started, God helped me. It was a breakthrough in my life; I had never before and have never since read aloud from the Bible at a racetrack—I have never since felt that God was asking for this.

That day marked the most successful winning spell in my career; a 55-year-old record was broken. When I read the Scripture, I made it clear that God had been the source of my victories. Winning is wonderful, but even better when you know why. When I won the AJC Derby not long after, I quoted (but did not read) another verse from the Bible in my speech that explains why: 'You can prepare the horses for battle, but victory resides with the Lord.'

8

SAINTLY

He rideth easily enough whom grace carrieth.

Thomas à Kempis, The Imitation of Christ

SAINTLY

In 1996 I was riding an exceptional three-year-old racehorse called Octagonal. The horse was a total heart-throb, the honeymooners' racehorse. The punters loved him. He breathed new life into racing. Riding Octagonal I won the Triple Crown (the major three-year-old races in Australia including the AJC Derby, Rosehill Guineas and the Canterbury Guineas).

But there was another young heart-throb on the scene, too—a horse that always seemed to run second to Octagonal. That horse was Saintly. This champion gelding seemed destined to always play second fiddle to the world-beating Octagonal.

Octagonal was owned by the Inghams and trained by John Hawkes. Jack Ingham rang me one day to ask me to ride Octagonal in his four major races for 1996—the Canterbury Guineas, the Rosehill Guineas, the Mercedes Classic and the AJC Derby. I had been riding another exceptional three-year-old, Filante, but because of my long and close association with the Inghams, I agreed to leave

Filante and take up with Octagonal.

As well as working with the Inghams, I also maintained a close association with Bart Cummings. I was actually riding Saintly every morning—John Hawkes was based at Warwick Farm, Bart is at Randwick, and I was living in Kensington, so for convenience I rode track work at Randwick, and so ended up doing most of Bart's track work.

I won my next race on Octagonal, then I went with Saintly to Melbourne to compete in the Australia Cup, which we won by a good three lengths—he romped home, steam-rolling the opposition. Bart tried to persuade me to continue riding Saintly throughout the autumn of 1996, which would have meant dumping Octagonal and the Inghams. I told Bart that I had made a commitment. 'I can't go against my word, Bart,' I said. 'It wouldn't be right. I've told Jack and Bob that I'll rode Octagonal for the autumn.'

Bart's reply said everything; he is a master arm-twister. 'I think you're on the wrong horse,' he said. 'This one's good. You're missing out.' Bart could talk the Devil out of Hell. But I had to keep my word.

On my next ride, I won the Rosehill Guineas on Octagonal, beating Saintly, who was ridden by Paddy Payne. As an autumn three-year-old, Octagonal was unstoppable; nothing could run him down. He had legs, pep and power—more muscle than any other horse in the field. Then Octagonal won the Mercedes; Saintly finished way back in the field. Finally, we rode the Derby. Saintly hit the lead at the 200-metre mark, but Octagonal wore him down and pipped him by a nose on the line—he was just too big and too strong.

During winter, both horses went out to pasture for a spell. The Inghams asked me to continue with Octagonal in the spring. They planned to send Octagonal to Melbourne for the whole spring racing carnival. If I were to go with him, it would mean an enormous amount of time spent in Melbourne and sacrificing all my Sydney rides. At this point, I was spending no time with Octagonal apart from race day, but I was still riding Saintly every morning. I had no idea what to do, so I prayed about it. God told me to ride Saintly.

I rang Jack to tell him my decision. He nearly fell out of his chair. He could not believe I would do that; it made no sense, in racing terms, to leave a champion three-year-old to ride a horse we had been beating consistently. What could I say? Saintly was the underdog all right.

I started riding Saintly in Sydney in the spring. He won a few races, and Bart made it clear that I had the ride for the Melbourne Cup. 'That's the big one,' said Bart. 'That's what we've got planned for him. We're getting him ready now.' Saintly's next runs were to be the Craven Plate and the Metropolitan, a Saturday and Monday double.

We thought it would be simple to run him on the Saturday in the Craven—there were only five runners in the race. We'd pick up $60,000 for an easy track work gallop. But it didn't work out as planned: Shane Dye rode the race of his life on a horse called Adventurous, and he beat us. It was a weight-for-age event, and Adventurous was a three-year-old with little weight, whereas Saintly was carrying a lot. He just stalled under his burden.

The following Monday, Saintly was beaten again—in the Metropolitan—and I began to have doubts about the wisdom of my decision. The Craven had been a hard run, and having to back up for another race only two days later, he struggled. This was less than ideal Melbourne Cup form. We all became gloomy. I doubted whether he could run the 2600 metres—let alone 3200 metres—for a major race.

Then I got an SOS call from Jack Ingham—he wanted me to ride Octagonal, because his form was slipping. There had been three bad performances in a row, and the Inghams were worried—more and more of their stud fees were flying out the window with every bad run. Octagonal's value was steadily plummeting. I went to Melbourne for the Underwood, and we won. It was the only race Octagonal won in that campaign, but at least it was a group 1 event, and the win did arrest the decline in his value.

Saintly's poor performances, on the other hand, were easily understood. He was an immature three-year-old—gangly, spindly and ungainly, like an overgrown infant. There was no question that he would mature, but it would take a little time. Given six months, I knew the dam would burst, and he would be unstoppable—he would spill success everywhere he went. Until then, though, he could remain the awkward teenager of the track. Nevertheless, Bart was cooking him to perfection, and he was a delightful, if unready, horse.

Bart decided to run him in the WS Cox Plate, in order to get him moving for the Cup. The Cox Plate was ten days away, and the pressure was mounting daily. Bart started to freshen Saintly for the 2030-metre race, getting him ready to run.

I flew to Melbourne to ride him and we stayed at the beautiful Como Hotel, which is owned by Saintly's owner,

Dato Tan Chin Nan, a Malaysian businessman. To everyone's surprise (except perhaps Bart's), Saintly won the Cox Plate. There were a lot of other horses making the running, but I sat back until we moved up the hill. Then I had the last shot. Four horses crossed the line together—Saintly on the outside, Juggler, All Our Mob, and Filante on the inside. But Saintly pipped the field by a short half head.

Saintly's win was testimony to the greatness of Bart Cummings. To be able to reverse his training preparations on a horse at short notice, get him ready for a major race against world-class opposition, and then get him first to the post in the race falls under the dictionary definition of incredible. The man is a genius.

And how did I feel? Well, winning the Cox Plate was right behind winning the Melbourne Cup in my list of lifelong dreams, so it was a real treat. It is the weight-for-age championship of the world, and run only by selected and invited horses. Those entry qualifications set the race apart: it is only for the best horses and the best jockeys.

I had almost won it in 1991, on Super Impose, but we were pipped. And when Super Impose finally won the race, in 1992, I was in Hong Kong. At the time I thought that was it. My best chance had gone. If I had been in Australia, I thought, I would have won the race—that is exactly the sort of thing jockeys tell themselves to get to sleep at night!

I could hardly believe how much Saintly had improved. Bart had him humming along with awesome power and throughout the whole period after the Cox Plate and leading into the Melbourne Cup, the horse just got better and better. You could feel it. I wondered what was going on—he was kicking like a champion.

For a few days I thought it was all a bit over the top. Bart was putting Saintly through belligerent, lengthy gallops in training. He galloped for 2000 metres, sometimes even for 2200 metres. He galloped him on the Tuesday, the Thursday, and the Saturday before the Melbourne Cup. But the horse never yielded; he kept pounding out the ground like a euphoric express train. His power and motion were explosive.

I came home one day that week and said to Kim, 'I think we've got a real chance here. This horse is unstoppable.' That was my opinion, but there were more than a few nay sayers around. A lot of armchair critics believed he was suspect over the distance; after all, he'd never run as far as that before.

Bart galloped him again on the Monday at even time (three-quarter pace) over 2000 metres. To the untrained, that might have seemed like suicide—the race was the following day. But Bart makes few mistakes with his horses. And the moment we hit the 1000-metre mark on Monday, I knew that Bart was spot on with his preparation: it took every ounce of my experience and strength to hold the horse back. Saintly had become a rampaging machine. He was ready.

Come Cup Day, I rode track work at Flemington in the morning and then went back to the hotel for a snooze. I came back to the track at 10.30 and had a sauna. I rode a few of the races before the Cup. The media seemed omnipresent—everywhere you showed your face, a media scrum developed. It was safer to hide indoors!

The Cup is generally the seventh race. There is an interlude of about an hour after the fourth race; it is filled with fashion parades and the like, and really sets the mood for the Cup.

Coming up to the race, I followed the same procedures that I had for every race in my career. Riding for Bart Cummings, though, you get used to doing things differently. Bart never, ever says whether he thinks the horse has a good chance. (I suppose he has been down that road too many times!) He rarely gives instructions about a ride. Other trainers are long on instructions, but Bart has confidence in you. He tells you to ride the race the way you see it, but to keep the horse in a good position and out of trouble—to do your best. I was my own boss, and it was up to me to make it happen. I was confident, but not over-confident.

Having learnt from experience, I know that if you enter a race of that quality without the proper mental and emotional humility, you will fail. If you lack appreciation for the subtle things, you will lose, because it is the small things that will win you the race. You have to go in confident and positive, prepared with a couple of race plans, but you must never get cocky—do that, and failure is a certainty.

We drew an inside gate, and we had a dry day. (Bart and I had prayed for a dry track, because Saintly hated the wet.) Everything was right for us. I used to be a superstitious jockey, but when I became a Christian, I gave up all that. Now I knew that only one power in the universe decides who wins or loses.

As usual, the stewards gave their warnings. The whole of Australia waited with bated breath—this is the big race, after all, the nation's race. Then we headed out of the jockey's room.

Going out to mount, the crowd was deafening. That

can upset a horse. It is not what people say—a few quiet ales can produce comments that are pretty colourful!—it is just the sheer volume of sound. All of it—the cheering, the booing, the flower-throwing, the comments—merges into a vast tapestry of sights, sounds and colour, a tapestry that makes Cup Tuesday something extra special.

Despite the fact that the crowd is like a football audience, and you see and hear things that you will never come across anywhere else in the world, you have to remain focused. Composure and self-control are your true allies. These are what will win the race for you. This is the ride of your life. If you let the razzamatazz get to you, you will surely fail.

Many horses were spinning out because of the noise and disruption, but Saintly was relaxed and ready, preserving energy. I sang 'Horses' to him, and a few Christian songs, and whether that helped him or not I don't know, but it definitely calmed me. His manner was relaxed and easy and ready to run.

Saintly jumped out of the gate like a jack-in-the-box, and because of his size and strength, I was able to push him immediately into the race. Out of the straight the first time, the horse was going easily, but halfway into the race, he started to pull hard, so I had to steady him. He was getting too anxious, and I had to calm him down with my voice. If you roar too much—particularly at other jockeys—you only stir your own horse up more, and then it will want to run faster.

The Cup is a two-mile event, but a particularly fast one. There is approximately 1000 metres of straight at Flemington before the riders first round the winning post. That always guarantees a quick start. We all barged out hard, and I kept Saintly to the fence the whole way. His size and strength kept him in his place as we rounded the winning post for the first time. From that moment on, he would be in the race the whole way. In fact, we held our ground at sixth or seventh for almost the whole race.

I let Shane Dye's horse, the Gai Waterhouse-trained Nothin' Leica Dane cross in front of me, so that I could follow him. Shane was third or fourth, but close to the front nearly all the way, so I knew it would pay to stay on him. The pace was fast for the whole race, and because Shane's horse was one of the better three-year-olds in the race, sticking with him was a good sign for our position in the field.

Despite the imposing size of Flemington racetrack, sometimes you can get boxed on the rails—trapped in a pocket—and never get out. The swoopers just keep coming past you, and you find yourself stuck, no matter how good your horse is. At the 500-metre mark I had the chance to get off the rails, so I took it. I moved to four off the rails—it took us two strides to hook out without causing any interference.

Now we were off the rails and only three lengths off the lead. It was a great feeling to be on a horse like Saintly—he was so close to the front, and he still had plenty of petrol in the tank. I could feel the power coursing through him; he wanted to roll the opposition. I knew that as soon as I released the reins, he would explode away with electric pace, leaving the others wondering what had just happened. That's how much acceleration he still had to give.

I slipped up on the outside of Nothin' Leica Dane, having watched him do all the work so far. Between the

DAYLIGHT AHEAD

500- and the 300-metre mark, we slipped into second position. I waited patiently. I could not believe how easily Saintly was doing it, particularly given the class of the race. Most horses were off the bit at this stage, but Saintly was taking it easy. He was racing to his work pattern.

I knew that if I let him go too early, something would come past and swoop on us, so I held him back until the 270-metre mark. Then I let the reins loose (the equivalent of hitting the accelerator on a car), and with three or four breakneck strides, he was gone. In a few short, sharp, power-packed seconds, he had out-distanced the field by three or four lengths. We blew past Shane Dye, who was nailed to the fence. Saintly never let the gap diminish—he finally won by a good three lengths.

We had spent the whole race, until the 500-metre mark, on the fence, which means that for 2700 metres, all we did was go forward. We didn't pass another horse for that entire period. But the last 500 had been wonderful. We blew every other horse off the racetrack that day—and they were quality horses, too.

I felt absolutely exhilarated when I crossed the winning post. When I won the first Melbourne Cup, I waved my whip in the air when I hit the post, and was fined $200 for that, so I refrained from any tomfoolery for two strides after the post this time. Then I let loose, waving my arm and pumping the air like a madman. The feeling is impossible to describe.

Sixty million viewers tune into the Cup worldwide, and they witnessed one of the great races that day at Flemington. Saintly showed his true pedigree before the eyes of the world. Everyone also heard me thank God for what He had done for us—that went over the airwaves into millions of homes—for which I am also thankful. God allowed His name to be proclaimed in racing through me, and through a horse called Saintly.

Many people rang me and wrote to say that they had not known I was a Christian and to encourage me.

Bart was, of course, over the moon. Saintly's win was his tenth Melbourne Cup; that statistic, in itself, demonstrates what a juggernaut of racing Bart Cummings is. You can't argue against ten wins, and no minnow ever wins the Cup—not even once. Maybe, without Darren Beadman, Bart would have won only eight. But then again, perhaps another jockey could have brought both Kingston Rule and Saintly home. Without Bart, though, I would certainly have won zero Melbourne Cups. Ten Cups is a remarkable feat, and I will predict here and now that Bart will go down in history as the Cup's undisputed king.

Bart was excited. His hands were trembling and his face was a picture of pure joy. To say he was overwhelmed does not do justice to his emotion. His eyes said it all. They were full of pride and affection for that tenth Cup.

I had very little riding gear left after that day at Flemington. Every man and his dog asked me for a whip, or a shirt, or a saddle—just about anything that wasn't nailed down! I also lost my saddlecloth. The whip went to charity—it was the one I had used to win the Cox, too—and in the end it raised $14,000 for street kids.

After the race, we went back to the Como Hotel in Melbourne. Dato Tan Chin Nan took over the main room in the hotel's restaurant, and a huge party followed. Chin Nan invited many of his friends, and later that night we ended up all standing around singing Waltzing Matilda. That party never missed a beat.

The difference between my first Melbourne Cup and my second one ran a lot deeper than just the names of the horses, the track conditions, the owners, or the opposition. The difference was God. With the 1996 Melbourne Cup I knew where my blessings came from. In 1990, I had raced on the strength of Darren Beadman; in 1996 I raced in the strength of my God. The difference was like night and day. The 1990 Melbourne Cup led to Hong Kong—1996 took me elsewhere.

* * * * *

After the Melbourne Cup, Bart took Saintly to Japan to compete in the Japan Cup. In Japan his work was even better than before the Melbourne Cup; he just kept getting stronger and stronger.

The day before the Japan Cup we worked the horse again. I spent the morning at the track with Bart and the horse. Saintly was hot. You could feel it. His work was phenomenal. The clockers and reporters were saying how good the horse was, that his times were amazing. I was more confident about the Japan Cup than I had been about the Melbourne Cup.

But there was one fact of which I was ignorant: the horse was on antibiotics for an infection. He was sick. When the time came for him to be taken off the antibiotics, he became sick again. The infection had not cleared.

I was dressed and ready for the track when someone knocked at the door. This was around five in the morning. I opened the door and it was Bart's wife, Val, dressed in a nightie and telling me that Bart wanted to see me in his room. My first reaction was that Bart was sick. What's wrong with Bart? I was wondering. I didn't give a thought to Saintly.

I got to the door of Bart's room. 'Come in,' he said. 'Would you like a cup of tea?' There was Bart in his striped cotton pyjamas, his thick mane of silver–grey hair flowing back from his weary brow.

'What's wrong?' I asked, thinking that Bart looked fine.

'We're out of the race,' he said.

'What?'

Bart went on to tell me that Saintly had been really sick; he had nearly died that night, and still no one was sure that he would pull through. I was in shock.

I had to ride that day in another race, so I still went to the track, but it was a huge shock for me. Saintly meant a lot to all of us. Fortunately, we found out later that day that he pulled through and would get better.

We came home from Japan and I waited to see what Bart would do with Saintly in 1997. I believed that Bart would race him in the spring of that year, but I had no idea he would bring him back as early as the autumn season. 'We're going to run him again in the Australia Cup,' said Bart.

We ran him first in the Orr Stakes at Caulfield. It was a 1400-metre race. The only thing he had done before that was a barrier trial. We were cruising around eighth or ninth for almost the whole race. The other horses headed us off at the corner and out-sprinted us, but at the 200-metre mark I put the pedal to the metal. Saintly mowed them all down and blew them away—he won by a couple of lengths, still heading away.

Things looked awesome for that season, but, sadly, the horse sustained an injury. Saintly bowed an off-fore tendon, and that saw him drop out of racing. He had all the right medical treatment, including laser surgery, and made a brief comeback in 1998, but after an injury was retired and is now out in the paddock.

It broke my heart when Saintly broke down—this was a horse with a beautiful spirit and a magical temperament. He had a softness about him, an intangible, special quality that made him almost human. He was as kind as a kitten, and didn't have a bad bone in his body. I patted Saintly every day after track work, and he cuddled up to me and lay on my shoulders and arms. He was a lovely, placid horse.

On race days, the strappers used to have to drag Saintly around the enclosure because he was so lazy and lethargic. But that was just a part of his gentle, quiet spirit. (Look at good athletes—they often seem very reserved, switched off. Sometimes you wonder if they are alive! They are generally in another world, saving oxygen and energy for what really counts.)

But like any good athlete, as soon as Saintly found himself in a barrier, he switched on like a Formula One racing machine. He was hot-wired and ready to burn rubber against the best in the world. (Octagonal was like this, too. He won by short half-heads, noses, and bare inches—heart-wrenching stuff. And just ask American sprinter Michael Johnson: you only have to win by a nose. The key is to just get there.) These horses are athletes, and they should be given credit as that.

After retiring on Boxing Day 1997, Saintly has been the one horse I have ridden. I went to Princes Farm to gather material for my regular *Sydney Morning Herald* article, and the foreman, Smokey Dawson, asked me if I would like a ride. Would I? I didn't need to be asked twice. The horse eventually appeared on the front cover of *The Herald's* new racing section—'The Form'—when it was launched.

Saintly means a lot to me. With a name like that, you have to believe that God has a sense of humour. (Saintly is out of a mare called All Grace, and his sire was Sky Chase. Need I say more?) No one could have guessed that a committed Christian jockey called Darren Beadman would end up riding a horse called Saintly! A lot of money was made, though, by joining those dots. After all, punters are superstitious, and a Christian jockey on a horse called Saintly is a good omen, if you think that way.

I can't really separate the three greatest horses in my life: Saintly, Octagonal and Super Impose. I can pick no favourite, because they have all contributed to my success. They all gave me great joy and great pleasure. But Saintly was the one that was there at the end of my career.

Saintly and Octagonal were the two horses that brought people back to the racetrack. There was a period in the late 1980s and early 1990s when racing attendances dwindled—people lost interest in punting on the track—but these two equine heavyweights dragged people in from the highways and byways and gave new life to the sport. They got the younger generation interested in the sport, and you can ask for no more than that.

Octagonal is now going on six, and his better racing years are over. Four- to five-year-olds are probably the best racing animals. If lightly raced, a horse's career might stretch to six or seven; Super Impose was an eight-year-old when he won the Cox Plate, but he was a lightly raced horse.

* * * * *

After winning the 1996 Melbourne Cup on Saintly, I continued racing through the autumn of 1997. I even won the Golden Slipper again, this time on Guineas. Little did I know, though, that this would be the beginning of the end for my racing career, the start of my swan song. By year's end I would be no more than a memory to racing. The fat lady was clearing her throat, and it would all end on Boxing Day 1997—Darren's Day.

9

WHY?

Have you got a second opinion on this matter?

BART CUMMINGS,
ON MY ANNOUNCING MY RETIREMENT FROM RACING

WHY?

Can anyone ever hope to explain their actions in a world of competing values and various beliefs? We do not know why some things in our lives happen; they just do. Sometimes it seems futile to even ask why, but it is a question that each and every person needs to address.

Many people wonder why Australia's leading jockey—a man who worked so hard to reach the top—would suddenly, deliberately, and apparently without difficulty, walk away from it all? Why? I had achieved what most Australians long for: security, fame, income, and success. Why walk away? Why leave it all behind?

Of course, no rational human being ever makes a move without proper consideration or some unexpected change in their life. Due diligence is required of any new venture. In my case, the amazing things that God did in my life throughout 1996 and 1997 led directly to my decision to abandon racing in favour of ministry training.

It all started on a trip to Toronto in September 1995 to see the revival at Toronto Airport Church and witness the work that God was doing here in people's lives. It was a crucial time for me as I had only just returned to riding after the disqualification; my heart was soft, and my eyes and ears were open to God. But there was some sacrifice in taking this time off: I was relinquishing many important spring carnival rides. Many racing people thought it was madness—well-nigh suicidal for my career if I was serious about making a comeback.

But I felt my spirit within urging me to go, that to forgo this opportunity would be a serious misjudgment. And so it turned out. At the Toronto Airport Church, I saw first-hand a true Christian revival—an outpouring of God's spirit upon humans. I had never seen such a welling-up of emotion: people laughing, people crying, and people enjoying encounters with the life-breathing Spirit of the Father. The whole experience was awe-inspiring as I was not used to spontaneous outpourings of emotion. It felt so genuine, so good and cleansing, that I could not dispute the integrity of it.

When I first walked into the church for the revival meeting, it felt like I was walking very deliberately across a hot beach towards the welcoming surf. I stayed for a week of meetings, and as I moved closer to the sea, the greater was my sense of the richness of God's presence. First I dipped my toes into those spiritual waters, and then I waded out deeper and deeper into the all-embracing ocean. I sensed God's love deeply and truly.

After four days at the revival meeting, I felt that God's presence was filling me so full, I was drowning. That night, one of the ministers prayed with me, and I fell to the floor under the force of an awesome spiritual power. I was out like a light for some two hours. Two hours of intense emotion and spiritual development, when finally something just seemed to snap within me—like a cable snapping, releasing an unnecessary load. At the same time it was as if a glass shield that had separated me from God had broken away and I could reach through into a new openness to His ways. I actually felt the pieces of glass falling, not dangerous or sharp pieces, more like a shower of cool, refreshing rain. Then a window opened and in a moment of revelation God showed me what was in Kim's heart—the things that Kim loved and longed for.

I came back to the hotel and told Kim everything that had happened. She told me that she had been praying that I would begin to understand what God had placed in her heart. She wanted God to show me her heart—what she needed in her life, what sort of person she hoped I could be. She felt then that God had answered her prayers.

Then, in graphic and surprising detail, she openly spoke of the love and understanding that she desperately wanted from me in our marriage—the patience, time and tender communication that I had failed to give her so far. I simply had no idea. Above all, Kim needed me to understand her life, her experiences and her sufferings. Her childhood and younger years had been painful and traumatic, and more than anything else, she wanted me to understand and help her bear these burdens. Now that I had come to my senses, I wanted to do that more than anything, too.

After that day, I started to fully understand Kim and appreciate her needs as a mother, wife and human being. How strange that I had never really been able to do this before! My revelation now made sense to me, and made sense of our lives. Now I knew who Kim truly was and I could share her pain. We had been married for six years, but from this time we moved to a new level in our care for one another and a renewed love. I take no credit for this; it was truly God's work. Our hearts were now joined in a way that life's rough road alone could never have accomplished. Our relationship grew strong; it blossomed and flourished.

God spoke to me in Toronto about another vital issue, too: that one day I would serve Him in a greater way. I had no idea what that meant, but it sounded exciting. Though it was unclear what I should do with this information, it was equally clear that God was serious.

I returned to Sydney and sought counsel from my spiritual mentor, Pastor Frank Houston of Sydney Christian Life Centre. I explained what God had said, that I would serve in a greater way. He advised me not to tell anyone. For the time being to keep it between God and me and to wait. 'God will let you know when he wants you to serve him,' he said.

I followed his advice and waited. It turned out to be the best piece of advice that I have ever been given. Those plans could easily have been destroyed or trivialised if I had not kept those cards close to my chest and waited for the Lord to tell me when to play my hand. But I never doubted God's purposes for my life; from Toronto on I patiently waited for the next step to be revealed. During this time, I sought to grow and thrive spiritually, to ensure that I would be ready.

* * * * *

1996 turned into a wonderful racing season for me. I

won the Cup in November, and everything I touched seemed to turn to gold. But alongside my racing successes, my true joy and delight was now in my growing family. 1997 began without event and I raced in the autumn. Mid-year, I felt it was time for a fun family holiday and planned a trip to Disneyworld. Kim suggested we add in a side-trip to visit the spiritual revival that had broken out at the Pensacola Church in Brownsville, Florida. I wasn't terribly enthusiastic, but I couldn't deny her. She wanted a fresh taste of spiritual revival.

We went to the church the first night we arrived, and there was a prayer meeting on. We returned the next afternoon, around four o'clock, but were unable to enter the main auditorium because it was too full. Kim said, 'I'll go tomorrow and line up early to get us in.' I had no desire to line up at all, so I let Kim go, and the kids and I went to the beach.

We met Kim there later, and we did have a great service. The presence of God was real, and praise and worship went heavenward with power, but it was only later that night, when I was in bed, that I felt a stirring in my spirit.

Normally, when I wake up in the morning, my first desire is for the newspaper, but the following morning, I wanted nothing but the Bible. I opened my old, well-used, leather-bound treasure. Before long I knew I had to go to church. I told Kim, 'Sorry, darling, but I have to go to church—something is happening.'

I queued up at 9.30 in the morning with a scorching hot sun beating down on me. Three or four hundred people had beaten me, so I was way back in the line. I knew that I would still get into the main auditorium, but I had little energy to think about that because God began to stir my spirit. I felt breathless and sat down on the sticky, hot asphalt and waited. I have sweated in saunas virtually every day of my racing career, but nothing came close to the heat of that day.

As I sat on the pavement, God spoke in my spirit: 'Now is the time to serve me in a greater way!' My mind flashed back to the Toronto message, then it raced through my whole racing career. In that split-second review I realised that racing, though my passion, had the power to divert my resources and energy away from the Lord's will. I had to focus elsewhere. I sensed right then that I should read the Bible book called James. I opened it up: it spoke about faith and works, putting faith in touch with works and works with faith. This was a dramatic confirmation of the call on my life. When Kim arrived at the church, my face was glowing like a beacon. She asked, 'What has happened to you?' In a frenzy I shared my news—now was the time!

After the service, we went back to the hotel and pondered our situation. When should we make a move? Next week? Next month? That part was unclear. But I knew that I had to retire; I could not balance the two—racing and the call. Some might expect that I would feel sad, full of regret, at this point. After all, I was talking about giving up everything that I had worked for—the dream and the success, fame and wealth that came with it.

Actually, nothing could be further from the truth: from the moment in 1994 when I included God in my life, it all started to make sense. I had made a mess of much of my life until then, but God had sorted me out. I had no reason to doubt the good plans God had for my future.

WHY?

From where I stood, racing had been wonderful to me, but the plans for the future had to be better still.

* * * * *

Coming back to Australia, I was bubbling over like a pressure cooker; I wanted to get the news out. But I knew that if two weeks later I suddenly, mysteriously announced my retirement from racing, things could go awry. I needed some wise guidance, so I went to see Frank. He said, 'One thing I know about you, Darren. When God speaks to you, you respond, and just look what has happened in your life. The time has come to pass, but what you do is between you and God.'

It was July, and I was heading into the August spring carnival. I was looking forward to it, but one small thing was troubling me. I was so excited by everything else that was going on in my life that I was a tad unsettled, and that boded poorly for my racing. I knew that to race well and win, you must be at peace. But all I could do was my best, and so I did that.

Friends and new contacts started to help me organise a plan. That plan included first telling my family and close friends. In July I told about sixteen people—only those I could trust, because I wanted this news to be kept watertight. I knew that when the story finally broke, the media would be hysterical. One issue alone motivated me to do things properly and decently: I wanted God's name to be honoured above everything.

Bart Cummings was one of my closest friends in the world, and was one of the group of sixteen that I told in July. At the time, Bart was away fishing in Darwin, so I rang him on his mobile phone. 'G'day, Bart, it's Darren here.'

'G'day, Darren, how's it all going?' said Bart.

'Well, mate, well. Look, I've got some important news for you.'

'Yeah,' said Bart, and I knew that his ears had pricked up. People love news in racing. 'What's up?'

'It's probably going to rock racing, but I've made a decision to retire from race-riding at the end of this season.' The phone went quiet for five seconds. 'Are you still there, Bart?'

'Yeah, yeah, I'm still here,' came Bart's confused voice. Then he asked, 'Why?'

I explained to him the clear call that I had received. The phone went silent again for a moment, and then Bart came back with one of the greatest Cummings' one-liners of all time: 'Have you got a second opinion on this matter?'

I said, 'Who's privileged enough? Who am I going to go to that can outsay the Almighty?' We both laughed.

Then Bart said, 'Well, mate, it's your decision. I wish you all the best.'

And that was it. I hung up.

I would have to release the news publicly. How would I get the news out to the racing fraternity, punters and fans? Should I call a press conference? Put an advertisement in the newspaper? Go to a radio station? What?

I rang Johnny Tapp, Sydney's favourite racing personality; I knew that he was the right man to release the story with dignity. Tappy and I have been mates for years. We have never been really close, but we had often run into each other at functions or at the track, and shared a laugh or two. We got talking. 'Look, mate,' I told Tappy, 'something is happening, and I want to release it to you. I want you to be the one to break the story to the community and the public.' His ears pricked up, too. After all, he is a journalist, and no journalist gets many scoops in life.

Tappy's fingers must have been twitching. 'What's that, Darren?'

'I'm retiring from racing.'

He gasped and said, 'Hang on a second. You've just given me the best right hook I've ever seen. I'm on the ropes. I don't know what to say.' I had stopped him in his tracks! To stop a race-caller, commentator and journalist of Tappy's experience means I must have thrown the best punch I ever threw! So in Hong Kong I genuinely did throw my second-best punch! After all, Tappy is a wordsmith—there can't have been too many times in his life when he had been lost for words! He just could not speak.

I said, 'Tappy, I really want to give this to you and I want you to deliver it to people for me, maybe on your program. I consider you one of the most respected men in racing, and I feel it's right that I give it to you because of what you've done for me and a lot of other jockeys. This is something back for you. And it's a scoop.'

Tappy had helped me a lot during my career. It's easy to forget just how greatly people like Tappy assist you. When reporters and commentators speak, they help your career; they give you a leg-up. For someone like Tappy to mouth the words, 'And what a brilliant ride by Darren Beadman...' across the airwaves gives your career an incredible boost. Owners and trainers listen, and Tappy and others had been doing this for me for 17 years. I now felt that it was time to give Tappy something in return. This was my chance to be loyal to him.

I knew Tappy had his own afternoon program on Sky Channel, so I assumed that he would use that. But I could virtually hear the cogs in his brain doing overtime while we spoke. Finally, he said, 'No, mate, we can't put it on there. We've got to go national with this. Sky Channel only goes into pubs and clubs. We've got to get this into the family homes of Australia.'

On the following Tuesday Tappy arrived at our house with two cameras and a crew. He came through the front door and into the hall, followed by a virtual safari team lugging loads of gear. He said, 'Mate, this is a real thrill for me. The only time I have ever used two cameras was with Fred Astaire's wife.' I had no idea what I would have in common with her, but I smiled anyway.

He went on to explain the importance of two cameras. 'I don't know whether you understand the significance, Darren, but having two cameras puts you in the studio; viewers will watch your face and mine. No matter what I ask or you answer, the viewers will see it.' I had no idea what Tappy would ask—we hadn't prepared anything in advance. It was all off the cuff, and that increased the pressure. No matter what I said or did, people would see every gesture, every movement. But I need not have feared, because God was with me that day and helped me to answer everything with conviction.

When I look back now over that videotape, I know that I could not now repeat many of my answers to Tappy's questions—God surely helped me to give cogent, lucid answers. Tappy asked me about my convictions, beliefs, decisions, what it would mean to me and my family, and I answered every question honestly.

We also did some filming at my church, Sydney Christian Life Centre, which is an old, refurbished warehouse. Tappy met Frank and had a talk with him. After that we filmed at Randwick Racecourse. Tappy and the film crew finally pulled away from the front of our house eight hours later.

It was deathly silent all week long. No one breathed a word. Not a soul knew until the story aired on the following Sunday. This was unusual for racing—usually only one person needs to know for the whole fraternity to know when a scandal breaks. Racing is like that, but this was different.

There had been three crew members with Tappy at my house, and there were four more people at Channel 9, all in the know. Yet the dam held, and the story was not leaked—not even a drop. For five days there was silence. It was a scoop for Channel 9. If the story had leaked, I would have been disappointed, to say the least; it would have done a disservice to me and to my God. I wanted the story to be delivered with integrity so that people could not be able to make a mockery of it.

Tappy's racing show is on Sunday mornings, but he told me that the story would not be aired until the very tail end of *Sports Sunday* (5.30–6.00 pm), leading into Nine's 6 pm News. At the end of the morning show, Tappy said, 'Look, folks, there is going to be an exclusive story break this afternoon on *Sports Sunday*, and it is going to rock the racing industry. It's the biggest news since Phar Lap's death.' (That might have been a slight exaggeration!)

I was at home and I could imagine what people were thinking. I ran around the house switching off my mobile phones, but before I reached the last one, it rang. I said to Kim, 'You get that one.' I knew that press would be calling to find out if I was the story or if I knew what the story was. Channel 10 could still steal 9's thunder—their news was at 5 pm.

We left our home phones on, and Kim played receptionist all afternoon. There was a whisper around that the story concerned me, so people were calling and asking for me, but Kim told them I was out on a picnic— little did they know that it was out on the back lawn with the kids!

Finally it was 5.30, and the story hit the airwaves. It shocked the racing world. After that, I took phone calls and answered questions until midnight or later. The next day, the story was everywhere.

* * * * *

Why? Why walk away from what so many people dream of having? When I retired, on 26 December 1997, I had just turned 32. I had a wonderful future within my grasp. I had not yet peaked as a jockey; I was still learning, still growing, still maturing, and I had many more years at the top to look forward to. I like to think I still had more Melbourne Cups in me. And I could look forward to earning perhaps upwards of a million dollars a year for maybe another ten years. So why?

The short answer is that I fear God. I don't mean that God terrifies me; simply that I revere God above everything. I love God with all my heart, but I fear that if I do not stay in what He has called me to do, then I am not staying in His will. And if I do that, then I go back to the way things used to be—me living my own life on my own strength and on my own terms. I could not endure that again; I learned my lesson in Hong Kong.

* * * * *

On the day when my retirement was publicly announced, Channel 9's Ken Sutcliffe commented that 'You can't doubt his conviction and courage.' The feedback from people was all admiration; they knew that many others could not have walked away, that the desire for a security blanket would just be too great, and that, therefore, they would have ignored what they knew inside to be right. Many would have calculated the consequences, but I did not; I was focused on my conscience and the call that I had received.

I think that the average punter deep inside understands what I did in retiring. People know that money and success are not enough, and that selfishness can drag you away from life's real meaning.

That period between August, when the story broke, and 26 December—my last race—allowed us to get everything in order: our emotions, our finances, our lives.

Financially, we restructured our lifestyle. The two years leading up to my retirement had been my two most successful years on the track. My horses had earned winnings of $12 million, of which, as a jockey, I kept around ten per cent. That put us in a healthy financial position, but I knew that my income stream was going to dry up, and I had to prepare for that.

My career had literally been a million-dollar one, but I now was giving it up; my riches are not here on earth—

they are in heaven. I was never in racing to make money; I was there because I loved what I was doing. Riding was a passion, and I was fortunate that it also led to worldly success.

But in August 1997, I realised that I could not just walk away from racing and expect my finances to take care of themselves. I had not made enough from racing to never have to think about earning money again. I couldn't simply put my feet up and say that my investments were going to take care of us for the rest of our lives—they won't. But I also know that God is my provider. If I stay in God's care, I will never starve. When I walked away from racing, I didn't have a clue about where my future income would come from. But having done so, I can see now that God has provided for me in ways that my understanding and imagination could not have dreamed up then with media work for Channel Nine, *The Sydney Morning Herald* and speaking engagements.

The lifestyle that we had led as a family had been very comfortable. It wasn't flash, but if we wanted to buy something, we always could. It is the same now, but with one major qualification: previously we were unconcerned about money, but now we are careful and thoughtful about how we live. I have no desire to abuse God's goodness: God will provide for me as long as I use my resources correctly and wisely.

I gave up racing because it was important to me to have real, certain priorities. My difficulties in life have come not from any inability to set goals and work to achieve them, but from ordering my priorities wrongly. I made winning horseraces my number one priority in life; consequently, when that fell apart in Hong Kong, my life also fell apart. Now my priorities are God, family, and work—in that order.

That set of values is rock solid. And it has granted me the precious gifts of true happiness, contentment, and peace. Without inner happiness, life can be daunting and uncomfortable; it lacks purpose and flow. But the moment you get a set of genuine priorities, whole new vistas open up.

Family is but one example. No matter how kind or good you are, you will have few friends in life. You can count your lifelong friends on one hand. But your family is a different thing altogether: family is part of you, and will be with you through thick and thin. My family has supported me through my transition out of racing, and that has made things much easier for me.

My Mum and Dad, who love me dearly, were shocked by my decision to leave racing. They could not understand it, and they, too, asked that same old question—Why? When I told them, they struggled with it. But deep down they could see that I knew I was doing the right thing. Before that, however, Mum had come to visit me one day at Warwick Farm racetrack. I spotted her at the gate outside the jockeys' room and said, 'Mum, what are you doing here?'

'I just want to talk to you,' she said with a mother's concerned look in her eye.

We sat in my car at Warwick Farm and chatted. She was worried that my Christianity was leading me off in some crazy direction. I was in tears trying to explain to her the love from God that I felt inside. I told her that the puzzle of my life now had the missing piece and now it all made complete sense to me. But Mum found it hard to put the pieces together into any meaningful picture.

When I told them of my decision to retire, I took the opportunity to explain to them all about Darren Beadman, about the things that all my life I had kept from them and about what God had done for me. I was open about my feelings, and that gave them the key to understanding my decision.

Later, after the news broke publicly, Dad came to see me at home. We talked, and on the street, as he left, he hugged me and said, 'You have made the right decision, son.' That was positive and reassuring, and it told me that the Why? had been answered.

* * * * *

For success in life, it's important to have a dream and goals. There are no shortcuts. You have to be prepared to pay the price, but when you finally achieve your goals, there is a wonderful feeling of accomplishment. Your dream is a reality. Travelling all that way, enduring the pain, and overcoming the grief, the doubts, and the anxious moments, takes you to a new level of experience. The stumbles, the falls, and the failures lead to a higher place.

When you have a dream, you never look behind you. Achieving a dream somehow gives you a breather—time for reflection and looking back. You examine the failures and hardships, and you use those as tools to motivate you to go further, to excel more. You hang on to integrity and honour and courage, and you move on to a new dream. If you never hope for anything, where are you going in life?

But equally, there is a time to walk away from an old

WHY?

dream and to look forward, to seek a new one. There are new targets, new mountains to climb, new heights to scale, and along the way you take with you the stock of finely-tempered wisdom you have gleaned. (The school of hard knocks really does exist!) There is a time to let go of the past and to look ahead. But before that new road can be travelled, old friends must be farewelled, and old flames must be given time to reduce naturally to embers.

I had no idea how to bring about a natural end to my career. How could I know when the time was right? God gave me the answer in telling me to retire at Royal Randwick at the end of the season; Randwick was where my career had started. God always does things with fullness, never by half measure, and it was important for me to finish out the season, rather than quit in August when the story broke. During that last season, between August and December, I had the chance to farewell the sport that I loved. I am thankful for that opportunity because it was a strong umbilical cord to sever. Racing had been my life, and now it would all end magically on Boxing Day—Darren's Day.

* * * * *

I had no regrets about leaving racing, because I received a grand farewell. When I first retired, many people in racing had me 10-1 to come back, but after five months I blew out to 50-1, and I will probably be at 100-1 soon!

I am in my apprenticeship now for a different master. Racing was too time-consuming, and while I have never closed the door on the sport—it has been very good to me—I doubt that I could ever return.

One man tested me to see how serious I was about retiring: 'Would you come back for $1,000,000?'

I said, 'Nope. Not enough.'

10

DARREN'S DAY

Prayer is not asking. It is the longing of the soul.

Mahatma Gandhi

DARREN'S DAY

Darren's Day was one of the great days of my life. In my mind it will always be the day I said farewell to, and let go of, my first true love. On 26 December 1997 I had the privilege of waving goodbye to friends, offering a parting kiss to my love affair with the racing industry and recognising publicly my camaraderie with the punters who had made it all happen.

* * * * *

Early in 1997, I started to lose my desire for racing. I still enjoyed it, and my desire to win burned as brightly as before, but somehow I knew that things were not as they had once been. The passion that had brought me into the industry at the tender age of 15 seemed to be dying down. Of course, the intensity of my feelings for the sport had waxed and waned many times over the years; that is normal. But this time it was different: there was an uncertainty, a discomfort.

At first I thought it was just a phase that I was going through. 'Hang in there,' I told myself, 'and you'll ride this out.' And, partly, I believed that. As long as I was still succeeding, I could block out any negative thoughts or questioning. Indeed, I rode plenty of winners in this period. Nevertheless, I knew something else was happening to me.

Looking back now at that period, I realise that my feelings about myself and my future and what I should do with my life were already being moulded by God. I was already beginning to move away from racing. This would make the final break easier; when crunch time came, my heart would not be torn in two.

And when it was finally time to make the decision, I can honestly say that it was not a hard one. By that time, the passion burning brightly in my bosom was no longer for racing; it was for God. That fact, more than any other, gave me the freedom to let go. I didn't fear the decision; in fact, in the end I was eager to make it. Not because I loved racing any less: I am absolutely passionate about the sport, and I could easily have gone on riding for at least another ten years. But there comes a time to give up the reins and get down off the horse. I knew that tomorrow promised something better.

I liken my retirement to parents letting go of their children. You have the responsibility and joy of watching them grow, of growing with them and enjoying them until the time comes for them to move on with their own lives as independent young adults. And when they leave (which will not be for Kim and me for many years yet!), you need to accept that life has changed now, that the wheel has turned, and that it is a time for new beginnings. Children leaving is not a sad thing, but a natural one, and one most parents accept with grace.

For me, racing was where I grew up and matured. I laid the foundations and the bricks and mortar of my life when I was in racing, but now it was time to move on. And it felt like exactly the right moment—not a day too early, not a day too late. There was a season, a balance, a rightness to it all; it would have been wrong of me to fight against what was happening. Had I done that, my life now would be diminished—it has grown and matured through leaving racing, and I have benefited from a new, added dimension and a greater sense of fruitfulness.

Racing provides a useful metaphor. It restricted me pretty much to the rails. If you only do one thing with your life, then it is all too easy to get trapped in a pocket and never get out into the open spaces. Real growing and living happens in the open spaces, where you can stretch your legs over more challenging furlongs.

* * * * *

When Tappy broke the news of my decision over television, into homes right across Australia, people responded with a genuine and profoundly moving love and affection.

The season of great farewells began at Wyong—the scene of my first win, when I was a mere 16 years old. Observers watching the travelling show with some amusement referred to it, tongue-in-cheek, as the 'Beadman roadshow rolling on'. Indeed, it was like an endless roadshow, as I travelled from dusty course to muddy track, saying goodbye to the good people of racing. The farewells were too numerous to count.

My Wyong farewell turned into a dual-purpose event. Little did I know that Kim had arranged another little surprise for that day: Mike Munro snuck up behind me on the podium, with a big red book under his arm, and said, 'Darren Beadman, this is your life!'

To say I was startled would be a huge understatement! Following the farewell speeches at Wyong, I was driven back to Sydney in a stretched limousine for the rest of the show, and Mike and his team—plus my family and friends—told the story of my life.

More send-offs followed in quick succession. The Victorian Amateur Turf Club (VATC) lavished on me my first Melbourne farewell, at Sandown, where they gave me a big picture of Octagonal. That function gave me the opportunity to say good-bye to my Victorian racing fans and friends, and it also marked the beginning of a marvellous phenomenon—I won a race at every track that gave me a farewell! In the four months between August and December, I won at least one race everywhere I went, and believe me, that is hard to do! I am sure that no one let me win; after all, there is a lot of money riding on races (so to speak!) and I am not that nice a guy.

In my home town, the Sydney Turf Club (STC) put on a evening farewell at Rosehill, to give people an opportunity to say goodbye and wish me well. More than 600 people attended. Punters, owners, trainers, racing colleagues plus friends and family were all packed into the function centre like sardines, and we had a wonderful night. I did not get away until nearly 1 am because I signed so many autographs. The genuine emotion expressed by

DARREN'S DAY

people for me was overwhelming, humbling. I had no idea that my riding career had meant so much to so many.

At this event, the STC gave me a life membership to the Club. No jockey has ever been recognised with a life membership—it really was a great honour. To receive such generous acknowledgment showed me that in my racing I really had done something right with my life.

* * * * *

Throughout this period, the AJC were making preparations for their own, final, big bang. I had told the AJC that because my career had started at Royal Randwick, I wanted it to finish there, too. The wheel needed to travel full circle, and Randwick is, for me, the headquarters of Australian racing (sorry, Flemington!). The AJC told me to put my head together with the people in their marketing department to plan the day.

'What do you want?' the marketing crew asked.

'Well,' I said, 'the public are coming there to say goodbye, so I want to spend at least half my day with the public, talking and shaking hands. I want to be able to say goodbye to them.' I told the marketing people that I would only take three or four rides that day, so that I could spend plenty of time with people. I also asked for a marquee where I could meet people, and for show-bags for the kids.

'What do you want in the show-bags?' they asked, with quizzical looks.

'You know,' I replied, 'the usual—Darren Beadman caps, face masks, a booklet, posters, and a few novelty items that I could sign. I want the kids to get it when they walk in through the turnstiles.'

The marketing department suggested that, as well as everything I had requested, we run a best-banner competition. The person with the best banner would win a trip overseas. That idea turned out to be a ripper, and there were some very creative and colourful banners on display. All in all, the combination of these ideas guaranteed that Darren's Day would be a grand farewell. Preparations started in October.

Meanwhile, the Moonee Valley Race Club (MVRC) organised a function for me at Moonee Valley. This turned out to be my final send-off in Melbourne. The MVRC worked with the Flemington Club, and put on a fantastically successful day. Moonee Valley provided a marquee, where I was able to shake hands with lots of people, and they also arranged several 2-metre tall gift cards for people to sign as they entered. The warmth of the sentiments people jotted down on the cards is indescribable.

I had three rides that day at Moonee Valley: one over 2600 metres, another over 1000 metres, and the third over a mile. All were very different rides, and I was in various and assorted positions throughout each race, but somehow I won all three! The punters who backed me that day must have been ecstatic!

The last time that I walked out onto the track at Moonee Valley—my last hurrah in Melbourne—people cheered and hollered, but all of that was drowned out by a sudden and overpowering sense of loss. I stared back down the straight toward the Valley's big screen, which was showing clips of some of my famous races. Then they started playing Frank Sinatra's song 'My Way' over the PA—'And now, the end is near, and now I face the final curtain...' I felt a tear trickle down and run over my cheek. It was all vanishing.

I stood silently behind the barriers and thought about what had been my career, my love, my life. This was my last ride in Melbourne, this was the last time I would ever walk into these barriers—I couldn't stop thinking about these things.

It had always been nigh on impossible for a Sydney jockey to go to Melbourne and be accepted by the Melbourne public. Melbourne punters have traditionally only cheered Victorian jockeys, and Sydney jockeys seem to be particularly odious to them. To be loved and accepted by the Melbourne public created a real powder-keg of emotions in my gut; I could hardly breathe, and I had to swallow hard to fight back the tears now filling my eyes. I had never felt this way before; that day at Moonee Valley, the consequences of my decision to walk away from racing finally hit me. I truly knew what I was giving up, and it felt as if there had been a death in my family.

All the barrier attendants wished me well and congratulated me on my decision. I found that very touching, and it brought home to me another truth—I knew virtually everybody in racing, even the barrier attendants in Melbourne. I felt as I imagine every one who has ever left their job after 17 long, gruelling years of dedicated service must feel. But this was my decision. I had written my own dismissal slip.

Inside the barrier I put my goggles down so that no one could see me weeping. My stomach was in knots, but I wiped my eyes and said, 'Right! Get it together!' As soon as the gates opened—Bang! I pulled myself together and stormed out, hungry to win. I rode that race, on a horse called Accolades, with complete focus and intensity, and won.

The standing ovation was incredible. I came in, gave my speech, and thanked the boisterous, affirming crowd that greeted me. 'I did it my way…'

I had promised my saddle to a charity. They auctioned it, and the money raised went to help street kids. I gave my whip to a young boy in a wheelchair, someone else took my goggles—even my silks remained south of the border! These were not acts of any great generosity; they were merely small ways to give back to people what they had all collectively given to me. I have no idea how many autographs I signed that day, but people were lined up for hundreds of metres.

Yet despite all those autographs, there were more—the MVRC had told patrons that if they had anything more they wanted signed, they should drop it into a box and it would be sent to me. Oodles of parcels duly arrived. I have no idea how many items I signed altogether—there were posters, caps, T-shirts, you name it. Eventually, they were all signed and returned. The pleasure was truly mine.

That day I felt very empty, but I still knew that my decision to retire was the right one. There is such a thing as pleasurable sadness, I have discovered, and it is worth bottling. This is the sadness that comes with giving up things dearly loved as they are replaced by other things more greatly loved. These feelings can be kept as a sweet reminder of special times once yours and now gone. That is the real beauty of life: it goes on in one direction, with all events interconnected, and you never have to forget the good that was, as you enjoy the better that is.

DARREN'S DAY

* * * * *

Preparations for Darren's Day involved frenzied meetings, complex decisions, and continued negotiations on various finer points, but everybody concerned agreed that it should be a fun day, a tribute not only to my career, but also to racing itself. There were many other demands on me at that time, too—including media commitments and riding—and I found little time to rest. The media, in particular, seemed in an incessant state of hysteria over the story of my retirement; hardly a week went by without some new exposé about my impending departure from life in the saddle.

Despite these pressures, I kept answering the calls, because people wanted to know more. People had supported me faithfully for many years, and placed their hard-earned funds on my race rides—and you can ask for no greater commitment than that! In turn, I wanted the racing public to know why I was retiring, what I was planning on doing, how my family and I were coping with the winding down of my career. It seemed only fair to let them know whether I had any regrets and what I thought my future held.

Those last four months at least allowed people to say goodbye to me and to share their thoughts on what I had given them through racing. They didn't really need to say thanks, because I love the people involved in racing, and they had given me as much as, if not more than, I had ever given them. Racing people are special people, and racing is a special world. The people in it are great givers, great supporters. You see how kind and generous racing people are when someone is down; everyone digs deep to carry the soul that is hurting. At times like that, you know that you are part of a community, a community you can trust.

Ultimately, it is impossible for me to express how I feel about racing people; I very much want to put something back into racing, in the long term. I cannot yet say what that will be, but I hope there will always be a place for Darren Beadman around the horses, owners, trainers and jockeys that make up this unique and sometimes bizarre world.

Darren's Day, 26 December 1997, finally rolled around. The AJC had done lots of advertising, and the response was overwhelming. An average crowd for Boxing Day at Randwick was 12 000, but for Darren's Day, 20 000 people showed up. That outpouring of well wishing was a fantastic testimony to what the public thought of me; it was something I hadn't really expected, something I had not adequately prepared myself for. People came from all over Australia—as far afield as Perth, Adelaide, Cairns and Brisbane. The Boss, now retired, came along to enjoy the day and see my last rides.

It no longer mattered whether I rode a winner on Darren's Day or not. If I rode a winner, great, I would go out a winner, but if not, no matter. I was committed to only three rides for the day, so I knew that my chances of winning were slim to none. But as luck would have it, I won my first ride!

I had planned to go out third or fourth in that race, but because the pace was off the boil, I changed my mind and decided to lead. I led all the way and won for Bobbie Thomsen and his owner Sunny Yam, on one of his fillies. Bobbie had played a part in my career for so many years, and it was great to ride a winner for him on my last day.

Sometimes I wonder whether the guys were really keen to chase me in that one, but they looked as if they were, so I assume it was a fair dinkum win, and I am sure the stewards do, too.

My second ride was for Jack and Bob Ingham on a John Hawkes-trained horse. It was important to me to ride for Jack and Bob that day, but I only managed a third. Too bad for Jack and Bob!

In my final race, the Summer Cup, I rode a horse called Ask The Waiter, trained by my old mate, Ron Quinton. The horse drew wide, and I gave it my best shot, but I had absolutely no chance. I knew Ron would be disappointed; he regularly gave me his favourites, but I always seemed to find a way to lose on them. A lot of the horses were under the odds, though; the public was putting their money on me—it had nothing to do with the ability of the horses. When I finally trotted in and faced up to Ron, I said, 'Mate, it's taken me all my career, but I've finally got something on you!' We both laughed.

In fact, nobody who had been important in my career missed out that day. They were all present, and that also was a testament to the links that hold racing together. It is one big family—not always happy, but like any family, united nevertheless.

My feelings were not quite as sad as they had been at Moonee Valley; I had now had a chance to farewell the sport that had helped me become the man that I am. My passion for racing had slowly been trickling away, like air leaking from a slight puncture. Everything in my life had been leading to this day, and when I got to it, I was excited about the future and thankful, not regretful, for the past.

The separation from racing would not be painful

now. I knew that I had made the right decision. A vast inner peace had settled on me. I looked back over my life in racing and saw that the people I encountered then were meant to be there. Ron, for instance, had been there from early in my career—we had enjoyed that great confrontation, then a firm friendship, and now he was present to see it all end. There are no accidents in life, nor any stray occurrences or introductions. Ron was part of that great tapestry.

Tony King, the chief executive of the AJC, spotted me walking over to the marquee to sign a few autographs. He said, 'Well, Darren, you've performed your first miracle.'

'What's that?' I said with some surprise.

'You've brought twenty thousand people to Randwick on a Friday!' He was right: that was miraculous given that average Friday attendances at Randwick in recent years have been around 12 000.

The 20,000 who voted with their feet that day testify to the importance of sporting personalities being accessible to the public. Throughout my career, I had been determined to remain in touch and approachable; people need to know that you are a real person then they can trust you. People also want to know that you do your best in all circumstances, and that had been true of me. I think that these things, more than anything else, made the public warm to me.

The hallmarks of my career have been integrity and honesty; without these, a life is morally bankrupt and effectively meaningless. In racing they become cardinal virtues, because everyone is relying on you to do your best—and, with luck, to win. That expectation, that faith, is why I always prided myself on performing to the best of my ability, and I suppose it also explains why the experience in Hong Kong hurt me so profoundly and deeply.

It left a dark question hanging over me, like a scar that would never completely disappear—when you base your life on the right things, values you have been raised to follow, and then your integrity is questioned, there are serious repercussions for the inner man. Being labelled a cheat is crippling; you know the truth, but before the eyes of a judging world, you are condemned. And when nothing you say or do can save you from the vengeance of others, you feel next to powerless. It takes time to recover from a trauma like this. In my case, the experience also led to a holy encounter.

But all bad times flow into good times, and Darren's Day showed me that there can be forgiveness and redemption in life, even in the eyes of a world hungry for scandal. Nobody bothered about Hong Kong on 26 December 1997; everyone wanted to celebrate what had been an otherwise unblemished and successful career. For that I am eternally grateful.

Many people approached me on Darren's Day and told me that they admired me and understood what I was doing. They wanted to tell me that they found my conviction and principles uplifting, that my decision to retire had inspired them. Hearing people say that was of greater value than anything I ever earned from racing. You can ask no more of yourself than that others respect the way that you have lived your life and the beliefs upon which you have acted.

Thanks to the AJC, a Christian group sang a few gospel songs on the day—that may well be a first for an

Australian racetrack! There were various other speeches and gestures, as Randwick really turned it on for me.

But nothing could have prepared me for when the time finally came for the Club to honour me. The Club presented me with a large, mysterious-looking box. I had no idea what it contained, but it looked and felt impressive. When I opened it, I discovered, to my delight and surprise, a 150-year-old church Bible in a beautiful black binding. It weighed a tonne, and must have been hard to find. I was truly moved that the racing community had decided to honour me not with a golden watch, but with something they knew would be dear to my heart. A lot of thought had gone into that generous gift. It was the AJC's symbol of respect for my service to the industry, and it was beyond my wildest dreams. It is something that I will treasure and pass on to further generations as a record of, and a monument to, what happened in my life and to Darren's Day.

* * * * *

That Bible truly is a Testament, because racing has left me with a rich legacy to carry with me on life's long road. Racing gave me my manhood and taught me discipline, sacrifice, a sense of winning and losing, success and failure, communication, relationships, determination, and how to appreciate good things. But racing also taught me that there are longings in the human soul that a sport, or business, or success, or fame can never fulfil.

Racing has brought success both to me and many other people, but wanting success can be a very lonely mountain to climb. There are always problems, no matter how famous you are; the key is who are you when the chips are down. You have to know that you have resources inside that you can hold on to, and those resources are definitely spiritual in nature.

There is now a chaplaincy program in racing, and I hope that it is active—having been there myself, I know that no matter how successful you are in racing, you can always do with help and support. Perhaps somewhere, sometime, the racing industry will set up a counselling line for people in racing who need assistance. After all, no amount of money or success will save you if your marriage falls apart or you fail to cope with your success (or failure) emotionally. At those times, you need help: a friendly face, a hand to hold, a kind word. We all need emotional and spiritual support. Who knows? It might save a marriage. The ravages of the industry lifestyle have devastated many formerly solid relationships.

Ghandi was right: there are deep longings in the soul that must be responded to. Darren's Day is about that for me. It signed off a wonderful time in my life and allowed me to move on into those new waters of spiritual nurture and growth that I so longed for. In letting go, I embraced a new phase of my life, looking excitedly ahead into the mists that most of us call tomorrow.

11

TOMORROW

*There is no medicine like hope,
no incentive so great,
and no tonic so powerful
as expectation of something tomorrow.*

O.S. MARDEN

TOMORROW

Darren's Day was a Friday, and on the Saturday morning, I already knew that something was different. Saturday had always been a work day, a racing day, for me; on this morning I arose from bed, opened the shutters and stared out into the pre-dawn Kensington darkness. Now it asked nothing more of me than a yawn and maybe a hot coffee. I was not expected at the track; no trainer was waiting there for me; there were no horses to ride. My racing career really was over.

The human body clock is a strange, yet predictable element of our biological makeup. On Saturday, 27 December, my body was telling me that it was time to work for a living—all my physical triggers screamed at me to get to the track, ride track work, then return home for a pre-race sweat in the sauna. But my mind told me to be calm and rest—it was all over. I didn't have to go anywhere.

My family had all come to spend some time with us over Christmas, so that they could enjoy my retirement day, and they stayed for a few days after that. We had a barbecue planned for lunch that Saturday, and that first meal away from racing told me a lot about just how much I had controlled myself over the years in terms of my body and my eating habits. My life in racing had involved so much routine—the wasting, the harsh sweating in the sauna, the endless physical regimens to stay in shape. These things had become habits that I no longer questioned; they were a part of me. But now, over lunch, every time I took a mouthwatering bite of my juicy, fatty sausage sandwiches—something most Aussies take for granted—I felt guilty. In fact, I felt like that for at least three weeks. That's how long it took for my body to get out of the old routine, the rut that I had been in, in terms of my lifestyle, hours, and kilojoule intake.

I had eaten bad foods as a jockey. I could do it once in a while, but it invariably led to feelings of guilt and self-recrimination. I knew that it was incompatible with the lifestyle and career demands of my profession. It just wasn't worth it—a bag of crisps or a hamburger always meant more sweating in the sauna and more exercise. Throughout my entire career, I had lived as if there were a huge padlock on the fridge and the cupboard, and that to eat meant breaking the padlock.

Now, as a retiree from racing, if I felt hungry, I could eat—whatever I liked, and without painful consequences. The first three weeks were hard, but I gradually grew used to this new non-diet, and happily indulged myself. Looking at me today you will see a man who has put on quite a few kilograms; so many that one of my colleagues at Channel 9 told me, over the air, to 'stay off the pasta'! When I saw Shane Dye winning the Brisbane Cup recently, I couldn't believe how thin he looked, nor could I accept that my physique once resembled his.

In January 1998 I went away camping to Kiama, on the New South Wales south coast with Kim and the kids plus Mum and Dad and Belinda and her family. I had never had the chance to go away with the family before and just smell the clean air, away from the pressures of racing, so this was really something different. Now I had freedom to do these things with my family; before it had been impossible.

When we came back home, I spent a few weeks getting organised for an overseas trip, which I was taking with Pastor Frank Houston and his wife Hazel. At first I had thought he was going on a holiday, but as it turned out, Frank was speaking here and there across North America. I was pleased when I found that out, however, because it meant I could get some 'riding instructions' from a man who had been in ministry for 50 years.

The plane trip over was my first chance to get away from the hectic life I had been living; to be free from phones, interviews, media, and family and friends. It was good; I needed time on my own to clear my head and think about what I had done and where my future was leading. The plane trip, in giving me that time to think, confirmed what I had known on Darren's Day—I had made the right choice with my life, and my years on the planet would not be wasted. I knew that everything had turned out just as it should.

Our first pit stop was Toronto—back at the Airport Church—and I was Frank's assistant throughout our time there. That proved a good thing, because it gave me a healthy picture of what my new life would be like and took my mind off racing, the profession that had meant so much to me. It took me out of my known, comfortable environment and focused me outside myself.

After leaving Toronto, Frank, Hazel and I went on to the Pensacola church at Brownsville, where God had called me to retire from racing. I acted as Frank's chauffeur during that period, and Frank ministered to me, but what impressed me the most about him was that the man I knew in the pulpit of Sydney Christian Life Centre was the same man away from the crowds, the prayers and the pulpit. And that taught me another invaluable lesson— you have to be the same person both on and off the ground, you have to practise what you preach seven days a week, 24 hours a day.

In Pensacola a proposal came through to me by fax about doing an advertisement with Burt Reynolds for the NSW TAB, for which I would be paid handsomely. I prayed and I read Scripture, but I could not decide what to do, so I thought I'd ask Frank and get some wisdom from an older head. I dropped by Frank's room, explained what the issue was, and asked him to look at it. The following day I asked him about it, and he said, 'Yeah, what do you think of it?' If I had expected an answer, I was sadly disappointed.

Startled, I said, 'Frank, that's why I gave it to you, so that you could advise me and tell me what you think of it.'

And he said, 'Well, no, what do you think of it?'

So I had to lay my cards on the table. I said, 'I feel God is telling me not to do it because there could be people with a gambling problem. It's not that I oppose gambling, but I'm concerned about leading people into it. I don't think I should do it; it doesn't feel right.'

Frank said, 'I wouldn't have gone against you if you decided to do it. It was your decision and I wouldn't have told you what to do, which is why I asked you first what you thought. But I think you've made the right decision.' That was another example of Frank's character and integrity. He doesn't try to control people; he lets them find a balance, a happy medium, a way in which they can practise their faith freely.

So I rang the TAB and told them I couldn't do it, that I just did not think that it was right for me. The next day, as if to confirm my decision, an Australian man approached me in the church and said, 'Darren, I used to be a really heavy gambler, and that's why I really admire what you've done in leaving racing for the ministry. And you know what? I've been set free. I don't have that addiction any longer. Your stand has helped me.' The question put before me had been answered; I had made the right decision.

Leaving Pensacola, we moved on to a conference in New Orleans. Frank gave me the chance to share my story with the people there, and I witnessed a healing time among God's people. People were coming forward in droves, talking and sharing about what God had done in their lives. Some had travelled thousands of kilometres to get to the conference, and they glowed with inner joy because of everything God was doing for them.

We returned home to Australia in February, and I had a few days to kill before school started. During the four months when I was preparing for my retirement, I knew that I would have to do some kind of apprenticeship to fulfil my ambition and follow God's call to the ministry. All ministers, as I understood it, did some kind of preparatory study, and given my experience in racing, I knew that an apprenticeship was in order, wholly appropriate.

I could have moved straight into the speaking circuit and shared my story with people, but I felt that proper, formal training would help me make this transition between worlds smoothly and easily. When you build something great, it is imperative that you lay solid foundations—Theo Green taught me that—because you want something rock-sure, something you can rely on when things get tough. Ministry training would build those foundations for me.

I soon found myself doing 20 hours a week in college, which was not easy for me—even during the best of times I had been far from an A-grade student. In fact, I had left school at 15, not valuing school learning at all. I had despised school study—I preferred sports—and since I was cock-sure that I would make it as a jockey, I had long ago told myself that I would not need any education; horses can't count and trainers are not interested in Shakespeare.

I was wrong. Little did I realise how important education really is. What I had treated as a waste of time is in fact a crucial part of a person's life. But there is no use crying over spilled milk. Yes, I should have put my years in high school to better use, but I had not, and now I was reaping the rewards. As I began my classes at Sydney Christian Life Centre's Aquila College, I found I was a bit lost.

At Aquila I am one of the oldest people in the classes. During those first few days, it was all a bit unnerving. I had walked away from a million-dollar career to sit in a lecture theatre with kids almost half my age. It was a very humbling experience, but it reminded me of the importance of one of life's priceless gifts—the teachable spirit, our willingness to learn. Out in the workforce, as one of the top guns, I had become used to people emulating me—how I raced, lived, ran my business. I was used to being a role model, and now I found myself sitting at the feet of my role models as they lectured me.

I had a real hunger to learn about God, and in my first class I learned about 'pastoral principles'. The lecturer spoke about the shepherd and the farmer. This sounded like my type of theology—I had grown up on a farm and could relate to pastoral images and depictions of village life. To know that shepherds, pastoralists, and fishermen wrote the Bible gave me hope that I could master this material. In fact, it really tweaked my interest. I felt sure that they had travelled in my world, that they could sympathise with what it was like to walk a mile in leather riding boots. In that class I felt comfortable—as if I had already been there for a year.

The lecturer used the metaphor of the shepherd and the farmer to describe different ways of living. The shepherd struggles through life on the side of grass-bare hills and slopes, relying on God to supply all his needs while the farmer lives in the grassy valleys, where the soil is enriched by the morning dews and river waters. In comparison with the shepherd, the farmer has few worries. It all started to fall into place for me: we are the farmers; everything is at our disposal. We treat material things as idols. In less-fortunate places, people have to be shepherds, have to rely on God for hand-to-mouth subsistence. I knew that I wanted somehow to be a shepherd, depending upon God's sustenance.

After a month or two, however, I started to ask God whether I needed to slow down a little and take stock. In my first few months at Aquila, although I was spending much time in school, I could hardly keep my head above water with the study, plus the constant barrage of requests for speeches and attendance at events from people out in the community. I started to feel as if I was drowning.

So I decided to stop and reassess it all before I was too far down the track. My heart was right, but I knew that I needed wisdom, balance, perspective. Again, I went to Frank, and I told him that I wanted to spend more time in the community, to attain a balance. 'Because of where I have come from, and what I have been,' I said, 'I feel that I want to get out and share my story with people.'

Frank was very sympathetic. 'Darren, you've always been obedient and God has been with you. Do what you trust is right, because God has a plan for you in this world.'

With his encouragement, I cut my hours back to part-time, which was just as well, because in March, Kim went to England to visit her sister. While she was away, I looked after the kids, attended college four days a week, and fulfilled my other commitments. I had quite a few speaking engagements, and things quickly became a grind. Not having Kim there to help me showed me how much I needed her help and support. But I trusted God and kept going. Looking back, it was poor judgement on my part to take on those speaking engagements of course, but I was hungry to get out and share with others what God had done for me.

This desire to go out and speak first arose in me in the latter years of my racing career. I had developed a real interest in Australia's young people and felt that I had something I wanted to communicate to them about life, values, community, and love. I wanted to help young people, to show my love for them. A desire to serve in this way really started to grow inside me.

I was invited to speak to a Youth Alive Rally in 1996, to an audience of some 16 000 teenagers. I had been riding at Rosehill all day, so I ducked across to Parramatta and shared the story of my life with the kids. Seeing so many of Australia's young people massed at a stadium in Parramatta was something else—it inspired me, kindling an emotion that I had never experienced before. I spoke for seven minutes, and then the guest speaker—US author Tony Campolo—called for people to come forward, to respond to God's call in their lives. Some 2000 teenagers did so.

From my own experience I knew that those 2000 lives would be radically transformed. It had happened to me not more than a few years earlier at Sydney Christian Life Centre. It was exciting, and I knew that I wanted one day to have a career speaking to such audiences.

More speaking opportunities soon came along. In January 1998, in Perth, I spoke at the Franklin Graham Crusade, to an audience of 26 000. Franklin is Billy Graham's son, and to work with his team was an honour. That experience again highlighted my newfound passion for public speaking.

Through the college, as a part of my ministry education, I have had to speak at many high schools throughout the Sydney area. This is part of our ongoing schools' ministry, which includes music, drama, and testimonies about where we have come from.

At first I wondered how I could speak to young people; I knew that I was passionate for them, but I wasn't sure how to communicate, what to say. So, I decided just to be myself—to tell them where I had come from, what had happened to me in Hong Kong and when I returned to Sydney, about my encounter with God, and of my subsequent life in racing and my eventual retirement. At first I could not believe how riveted the kids seemed to be by my story, but I soon realised something about teenagers: they just want to hear the truth—loud, clear, and relevant. They reject lies, deceptions, and salesmanship; they want honesty, integrity, and forthright communication.

I knew that it was impossible to fabricate anything talking with them; they will smell a rat. But when you tell the truth, they thank you for it. The day that I spent at Caringbah High School led to 135 decisions to take up the call of Jesus and become His followers. Seeing the joy and delight on the kids' faces, feeling those eager hands hungrily pressing into mine, and their enthusiasm to hang around and talk, was every bit as thrilling as winning the Melbourne Cup. And the questions they asked were intelligent and passionate.

Not long afterwards, at the invitation of the Chairos Prison Ministries organisation, I was offered the chance to speak to some of the inmates at Sydney's notorious Long Bay jail. The meeting was set for a Tuesday afternoon, and on Tuesday morning, in class at college, I was still thinking about what I would say, how I would open the innings. I should have been thinking about the lecturer and his topic for the day, but my mind kept skipping ahead to the prison inmates—what would I say to them?

Right there, in class, God's Spirit sent me a crystal clear message: Tell them that I have come not to judge you but to love you. That afternoon, with some fear and trepidation, I arrived at Long Bay Jail with some college students who had come along to help me run the session. Long Bay is a grey, sullen, gloomy place. I sensed an evil presence. My heart felt as if it was locked in a vice from the moment I entered, and I was very nervous; I had butterflies in my stomach and my hands were clammy. I couldn't stop worrying about how I would speak to the guys inside and how they would respond to my obvious nervousness.

We went through into the jail, emptied our pockets at security, and slowly, deliberately, walked into the anteroom to the prisoners' training area. A guard explained the routine procedures to us, then we shuffled nervously toward the training room for an open ministry time.

Inside the training room the inmates, dressed in their drab, cheerless prison green, were receiving prizes for a contest, and their cheering and clapping were deafening. Some of them were enormous, hulking men, they seemed so aggressive. Some of the guys' faces were beat up, bruised, busted. For me, it was terrifying—my imagination began to run wild, as I tried to imagine what their lives, confined to these narrow stretches of concrete and steel, must be like. I shook a few hands, said g'day, and tried as hard as I could to hold normal, day-to-day conversations. But, the circumstances were just about as far from normal as I ever expect to encounter again.

I had brought along the video about my life, which includes much of the material from Tappy's interview. My student colleagues put on the video, but unfortunately it had not been rewound properly; the wrong half was playing. At the end I apologised to the group and explained that the video would run for twice as long as I had promised, and asked if they would mind that. They shouted out: 'Go ahead! We love it!' So we played the rest.

But the video had to end sometime, and all too soon it was my turn to speak to the men. I have no hesitation in admitting that I felt quite intimidated. With heavy legs and a nervous gut, I got up to speak. I had a really oppressive feeling. What on earth was I doing here? I wondered.

First, I thanked them for having me and then I proceeded to tell them what had happened to me at college that day: 'This morning I was thinking about you guys, and I was wondering what I would say to you because I've never been in a working jail before. But the Lord gave me something to help, and I'm going to tell you what it is. He said, "I'm not here to judge you. I'm here to love you."'

There were 180 guys present, and they started yelling with delight at the top of their lungs. It just about brought the roof down. Their enthusiasm immediately lifted the heaviness that I had been feeling, and a new freedom came over me as I shared my life story and God's love with them all. Over 20 guys responded to my call to make a commitment to Jesus Christ.

Later we met with the Chairos group in the prison—the men who had already committed their lives to Jesus Christ. I sat patiently and quietly with the group, and before long one of the men spoke. You can usually tell who the leader is in such circumstances—it's invariably the one who speaks first. I had no idea what these men had done to be locked up, and perhaps I did not want to know; it seemed to matter little.

The leader, imprisoned for who knows what offence, said: 'Look, what the media perceives, and what people tell you about jail—there's no truth to it. Let me tell you what jail is like: go into your bathroom in the middle of winter, turn the lights off, shut the hot water off—because you don't have that in here—and put a board over your bath and lie on it. That's your room for 18 hours a day. So just get a picture of that if you want to know what jail is like. That's jail for us.'

He said that it was so hard to get through to the authorities—'the boys in blue'—just how necessary programs like ours were for people in prison. He said that there was only one thing that would change people's hearts—God. He said, 'They just don't get it; only God will change our hearts. Not men; not rules. Just God.'

He went on to explain that his brother was heading down the same track that he had gone down. He told me that he kept telling his brother not to break laws, not to commit crimes. 'No one in here really understands where we are at,' he said. 'We know the truth, and the truth sets you free, no matter where you are. I'm in here for what I've done, and I have no problem with that, but now I'm coming from a different angle, and nobody gets that. God has changed my heart. As soon as the authorities understand that, they'll get somewhere with me and others like me who have accepted God. I love God,' he said.

That jail visit showed me another side of life. In the racing world, I only saw one group of people, but out in the big, wide world, I realised there is so much more. And God's love reaches out to all of them, to all sorts of people from all walks of life. Some may ask, how can you love someone you do not know? I do not need to know each human to know that I love them—because God loves them.

I believe that is where God is leading me. I believe that it will be my job to help care for others and to help meet some of their needs—no matter where they are, what they have done, what they believe in or hope for. For those young kids who are underprivileged and think that all hope is gone, that life has nothing to offer—I want to be there to offer a helping hand if I can.

* * * * *

Knowing this, finding this truth, I have started to drive a truck every second Thursday into Redfern to deliver day-old bread donated by caring businesses to the needy. This program is organised by City Care, a group affiliated with the Christian Life Centre. And driving bread to 'the block', in downtown Redfern has given my life a meaning in a way that I never had riding horses. I go for one reason: to show my love, to show these people that someone cares.

Kids come up to me in droves. They dress like American urban gangsters, in thick sports jackets, baseball caps and baggy jeans. They ask me what is happening in my life, what I am doing, what I believe in. And I share with them the love that I have found. They see me as a person who has travelled a long way from my days in racing, and I hope they see me as someone they can relate to. They know what I am doing; they know that I am a Christian—that has been well publicised.

I go to Redfern to show the kids there that I love them, to tell them that crime does not pay off, that they can make a go of it. I want them to believe in themselves and that they have choices, that drugs are not the only answer, that there is hope—a future.

I plan to go out more often, especially at night, to try to reach out wherever there are kids in need on the streets. This is my new apprenticeship. I realise that I need to understand their problems, to understand their world, where they come from, and what they live with. Without that knowledge, my efforts in Redfern will be just so much hot air. I want to build relationships with these kids before I take them somewhere.

Do I want to take them somewhere? Yes, I do. My future ministry, I believe, lies here, working with the street kids, who for whatever reason, need help and support. I can join only a few of the dots in the whole picture at this point, but I know that God is calling me to help the young people out there in need of assistance. I can now start to put together the pieces of the jigsaw puzzle and see my future career.

My future is leading me to these kids. I hope to grasp the details and contours of their lives, as I once wanted to master the principles of successful horsemanship. This is my second apprenticeship. I want to help prepare them for life, work, love, and compassion. I want to help them beat the drugs that are devouring their minds, hearts, desires, and gentle spirits. I want to help them overcome the pains, the sickness, and the injuries in their lives.

I recognise now that my call has led me here—to the street kids. Some go to the streets despite the love and care of their parents, but others are there because life has dealt them terrible cards. They have had no choice; they may have been sexually abused, or maltreated and thrown out. Most feel powerless to influence their own destiny. But love can give them that power.

Some of the kids have never known a home; all doors in their lives have closed in their faces; it's no surprise that they become antisocial. Too many kids on the streets are crying out for a true home. They want to find genuine affection and real care in the kind of safe, warm environment that so many of us take for granted. They want to find role models—mothers, fathers, heroes. Many of them come from fatherless homes, but I can tell them that there is a Father in heaven who loves them. There can be replacement fathers and new father figures.

Ultimately, the greatest gift that we can give anyone is the gift of hope. Hope that will let them lift their heads up toward a new day's sun and smile in expectation of better things. There is healing in life, a balm for every pain. I know. Kim and I have both experienced pain in our lives. Some of it we brought upon ourselves, but that matters little. What matters is that there is redemption, healing, and a future.

It seems to me that there are few easy answers in life. Pain does not wipe itself away, and tears will hang in our eyes until the time of redemption. For many people, a long and arduous healing process is needed. This is true for the kids on the street. Their hurts have damaged their spirits. Attempting to build relationships with them is difficult beyond belief. Many find it hard to trust again; to extend a hand and have it rejected is soul-destroying, and few try to reach out again.

You can lead a horse to water, the saying goes, but

you cannot make it drink. I want to help these kids learn to drink from the water of God. I see it as my mission to help lead the kids to a life that offers them more than a vicious cycle of drugs, depression and death. There is hope; there is redemption; there is a future worth fighting for. I want them to know and believe that God is not about church or religion—God is real, not a figment of our imagination, and God is about people. About love.

Church is important, because we need a place where we can come together for worshipping, strengthening, and growing, but ultimately the real needs are out there in the community. The majority of people are not in church; they are out there in the community, so we need to be there, too.

* * * * *

My future will continue to engage me with the larger community. I want that more than anything. Particularly, I want to maintain my links with racing. Fortunately, not too long into my retirement, I began working with Channel 9 on the Saturday Racing Show. This has kept me in touch with the industry for which I still carry a brightly-burning torch. Doing my regular spots for the show has kept me thinking about the players, the horses, and the industry that was once all I ever longed for.

I also began to write a column for *The Sydney Morning Herald's* 'The Form' in 1997, and I have continued that column; the editors tell me it has been hugely popular with punters. These two responsibilities, together with my STC ambassadorship—I helped promote the Autumn Carnival on television, at media launches and on the race days—have kept me in the racing industry, and my interest and passion have been able to continue to find productive outlets.

But more than anything, I look forward to a future of helping others find lives of relevance, trust, and meaning. If nothing else, I hope my story shows that there can be redemption after defeat, there can be forgiveness after failure, and there can be light where there was darkness. That is all I seek to offer.

My Hong Kong experience left me on the back foot, expecting no good for the future, but I was wrong. There is light after darkness, there is resurrection after death. The fall that appears life-threatening can lead to a more meaningful and fulfilling life if only you open your eyes and look further than today. Meaning never lies in the night; it always rises with the new dawn that is tomorrow.

EPILOGUE

*I go… to forge in the smithy of my soul
the uncreated conscience of my race…*

JAMES JOYCE,
A PORTRAIT OF THE ARTIST AS A YOUNG MAN

EPILOGUE

As I sit at home, six months after retiring, and reflect back over the last 32 years, I get a very deep sense of satisfaction: life has indeed been good to me. I have achieved many of my goals and dreams, and I have enjoyed myself along the way. My family is such a blessing and I am loving having the chance now to spend more time with my children—Mitchell, Jessica and Rachel—and watch them grow. The three of them are so close.

Over the years, there were many times when I thought that I would not make it—times when I thought that the odds were all against me. But I have come through into a special place—a lush, green track, from which I can assess all that has happened and look forward to all that will happen. I know that as I go forward, still relatively young in life's terms, I will take with me hands steadied by the tempering fires of experience. I will no longer hold so tightly onto the reins of my life; living with eyes of faith has given me true freedom—there is nothing to fear, nothing to win on my own, and nothing to claim my own.

DAYLIGHT AHEAD

There is a sense of true humility.

And there is also a sense of excitement, for I know that as I go boldly into the future that is prepared for me, I take with me a loving wife—someone I now truly understand, and who truly knows me—and three beautiful children, whom God has entrusted to us.

I never miss those early morning starts, or the sprints astride a sweating, snorting horse. I can sleep in, rise when normal people rise and eat whatever, and whenever, I like. Sometimes, though, when I drive past an empty paddock and see a lithe chestnut or brown stallion grazing peacefully on fattened shoots, something goes faster inside me. And I think back on the places I have been, the faces I have seen, and the pleasures and pain of winning and losing. You never have to fight your memories; you can just enjoy them.

I sit in my ministry training classes (a few kilos heavier) and I learn about things that will help me comfort others with their varied needs, and I know that life grows and changes as the years drift by. Somehow, the years never drifted by in racing, but I have a feeling that they will now and that I will enjoy the process.

Racing was all pace, verve, and get-up-and-go—and life is in many respects still the same, but I do different things. My speaking career is taking off. I am sharing my story with thousands of others in the hope that they can find something of the peace and tranquillity that I have found. I have new pressures, fresh races to run, and the maturity now to learn from them.

All in all, I am positive about what the future may bring. I left racing to go into ministry. I know that ministry means serving, helping, assisting. I want to spend the rest

EPILOGUE

of my time benefiting others. I want to show that there is love, hope, and care. People can change, do change. I want to help.

Where will it all lead? To a good place, I am sure. I never give up hope or tire of trying to open my hands to others. If through my years in racing, people feel they can talk to me and share themselves, then so much the better. I no longer live for myself, but for the God who saved me.

I began my life as nothing special, just a small weedy kid on the outskirts of Canberra. But I had a dream, and I had the self-belief to make it happen. Even so, without helping hands from others, I could not have achieved my dreams: without Mum and Dad pushing me on to ride; Mick Gavin telling me that I could be a jockey; Sharon Hasler's assistance; Theo Green, my mentor; or Bart Cummings. They all played their part.

Others have played a role, too. I have needed the guidance of Frank Houston, and I imagine I will need it more in the future. But mostly, I needed the intervention of God. My disqualification in Hong Kong truly was a time of darkness for me, and it brought me to my knees. But it also brought the realisation that I could not do it on my own. I needed help.

Today, it is all so much clearer. I have fresh dreams, and I have the love and support of many old friends, many new friends, and Kim and the kids. What more can any man ask for? That is all you really need to fulfil the tasks for which God made you. I want to win new races, and with God's help, I will.

When I hit the lead in the 1990 Melbourne Cup riding Kingston Rule, I saw daylight ahead. I see it again now.

And that is why I retired. It is time to pursue the other wonderful plans that the God who made me has for my life. The rush of enjoying each step toward that winning post is already unbelievable.

CAREER HIGHLIGHTS

CAREER HIGHLIGHTS

Apprenticeship Begins
January 1982—Randwick

First Ride
2 June 1982, Royal Sheba 12/1, Rosehill: second to Avon's time in Lilyfield Handicap

First Win
8 July 1982—Flagette 20/1, Wyong

First City Win
10 July 1982—Gaelic 6/1, Warwick Farm, Leumeah Welter Handicap (1400 metres)

First Group One
14 April 1984—Inspired, STC Golden Slipper Stakes

Apprentice Wins
147—Australia; 25—France

Apprentice's Premiership
1982-3—First (48 wins); 1983-4—Second (33 wins)
1984-5—First (33 wins)

Sydney Jockey's Premiership
1990-1—Second (91 wins)
1991-2—Second (68 wins)
1994-5—First (128 Wins)
1995-6—First (115 wins)
1996-7—Second (75 wins)
1997-8— (21 wins; retired Boxing Day 1997)

Four Wins on One Day
10 Oct 1990—Canterbury
20 May 1995—Randwick
19 July 1995—Canterbury
6 August 1998—Warwick Farm

Five Wins on One Day
27 October 1990—Rosehill
16 July 1995—Canterbury

1984 Golden Slipper Winner
14 April 1984—Inspired, second youngest winner (18 years, 5 months)

1984 (Group 1) Deauville Prix Morny Winner
(This is the major two-year-old race in France)

Winner (Group 1) AJC Epsom Handicap
1988—Regal Native
1991—Super Impose
1994—Navy Seal

Winner (Group 1) AJC Doncaster Handicap
1991—Super Impose

Winner (Group 1) VATC Oakleigh Plate
1997—Spartacus

Winner (Group 1) VRC Melbourne Cup
1990—Kingston Rule
1996—Saintly

CAREER HIGHLIGHTS

Winner (Group 1) VRC Chrysler Stakes
1997—Catalan Opening

Winner (Group 1) New Zealand Derby
1996—Great Command

Winner (Group 1) NZ JRA Plate
1997—Captain Moonlight

Winner AJC Australia Day Cup
1995—The Fledgling

Major (Group 1) Two-Year-Old Wins
STC Golden Slipper: 1984—Inspired; 1997—Guineas
QTC Sires' Produce Stakes: 1996—Anthems
QTC Castlemaine Classic: 1996—Anthems
VRC Sires' Produce Stakes: 1997—Millward

Major (Group 1) Three-Year-Old Wins
AJC Australian Derby: 1996—Octagonal
AJC Spring Champion Stakes: 1997—Tie The Knot
AJC Flight Stakes: 1991—Electrique, 1996—Dashing Eagle
STC Canterbury Guineas: 1996—Octagonal
STC Rosehill Guineas: 1996—Octagonal; 1997—Tarnpir Lane
STC Storm Queen-Ansett Australia Stakes: 1996—Saleous; 1997—Danendri
VRC Oaks: 1995—Saleous
VATC Caulfield Guineas: 1989—Procul Harum
VATC 1000 Guineas: 1996—Dashing Eagle; 1997—Lady Of The Pines

Major (Group 1) Weight-for-Age
AJC Chipping Norton Stakes: 1986—Heat of the Moment; 1991—Super Impose; 1992—Super Impose
AJC All-Aged Stakes: 1989—Card Shark
AJC Queen Elizabeth Stakes: 1988—Authaal
STC Rawson Stakes: 1991 Super Impose
STC George Ryder Stakes: 1995—March Hare
STC Mercedes Classic: 1996—Octagonal
MVRC WS Cox Plate: 1996—Saintly
MVRC Manikoto Stakes: 1997—Spartacus
VRC Australian Cup: 1992—Let's Elope; 1996—Saintly
VATC Futurity Stakes: 1996—Star Dancer
VATC Underwood Stakes: 1996—Octagonal
VATC CF Orr Stakes: 1997—Saintly
BTC Domben Cup: 1996—Juggler

CAREER TIMELINE

CAREER TIMELINE

February 1981
Joins Randwick trainer Theo Green as a 15-year-old

January 1982
Starts apprenticeship at Randwick, aged 16 years 2 months

June 1982
First ride

July 1982
First win

July 1982
First city win

April 1984
Wins the Golden Slipper Stakes on Inspired

1984
On 'loan' in France to expatriate Australian trainer, John Fellows

1985
Returns to Australia and completes apprenticeship

November 1987
First Ride in Melbourne Cup, 14th on Scarvila

May 1989 - September 1991
Accepts role as stable jockey with Vic Thompson's Crown Lodge

November 1989
Second Ride in Melbourne Cup, 17th on Palace Revolt

October 1990
Rides five winners in a day at Rosehill; receives call from Bart Cummings to ride the Melbourne Cup

November 1990
Third ride in Melbourne Cup, wins on Kingston Rule

1992
Wins the VRC Australian Cup on Let's Elope for Bart Cummings

September 1992–June 1993
Rides in Hong Kong for Australian trainer, John Moore

June-September 1993
Spends the off season in Australia

September 1993
Returns to Hong Kong to ride for Australian trainer, Neville Begg

November 1993
Disqualified from international racing for nine months

February 1994
Conversion to Christianity

September 1994
Returns to race riding in Sydney

CAREER TIMELINE

1994–1995
Wins the Sydney jockeys' premiership, 128 wins

1995–1996
Rides 11 Group One winners; only the eighth jockey to ride double-figure Group One winners in a single season

1996
Rides Octagonal in four Group One wins in the autumn season

1996
Switches in the spring from Octagonal to Saintly and wins Cox Plate

November 1996
Wins second Melbourne Cup on Saintly

August 1997
Announces publicly his intention to retire from racing

December 1997
Retires from racing